KNIFE MAKING

KNIFE MAKING

a practical guide

Owen Bush

THE CROWOOD PRESS

CONTENTS

1	Tools of the Bladesmith's Forge	7
2	The Bladesmith's Materials	27
3	Forging the Blade	35
4	Grinding the Blade Before Heat Treatment	53
5	Heat Treatment	63
6	Grinding the Blade After Heat Treatment	73
7	Making the Handle	89
8	Sharpening the Blade	99
	Index	110

CHAPTER 1

TOOLS OF THE BLADESMITH'S FORGE

THE FORGE

The basic tools that the bladesmith uses to shape hot steel into a blade are the forge, the anvil and a hammer.

We will start by looking at the forge, the means by which fire is used to heat steel to a temperature at which it glows and becomes plastic enough for the smith to forge it into shape.

At Bushfire Forge, the bladesmithing school I run in south-east London, there are two types of forge installed: solid-fuel forges and gas forges. Both types have advantages over the other, but also their disadvantages.

Solid-fuel forges

Solid-fuel forges that run on fuels such as coke, coal and charcoal tend to run hotter than a gas forge. This means that steel will heat up more quickly in a solid-fuel forge and so it can be brought up to the right temperature for forging in less time than it takes with a gas forge. For example, it may take 30 seconds to heat a piece of steel to forging temperature in a coke forge, but 90 seconds to heat the same bit of steel in a gas forge. This does not sound like a great difference, but that

Solid-fuel forge.

The author with hammer, anvil and forge.

extra minute every time you heat the steel soon adds up to more than a hour or so over a whole day.

All types of forge that burn fuel produce combustion gases, including the toxic gas carbon monoxide (CO), and I always have one or two CO monitors set up at the correct height in my forge area. It is therefore very important that your forge area is fitted with good extraction and ventilation equipment. A well-designed chimney, for example, should be enough for a solid-fuel forge, but in order to expel smoke and stale air up the chimney it is necessary to ensure that fresh air can enter the forge building to replace it.

A side blast forge fitted with a water-cooled bosh and tue-iron to regulate how much air is allowed to enter is the mainstay of a modern British industrial forge. A jacket of water surrounding the tue-iron prevents the fire from burning the tue-iron away. I would recommend using a cast-iron, water-cooled tue-iron since these can last for at least half a century if they are treated well and kept topped up with water. A cheaper bosh and tue-iron made from mild steel should last for more than a decade before it eventually rusts away. They are quite easy to make if you are able to fabricate steel. If you do not have the facilities, however, some good-looking fabricated forges are now available online.

Coke

I often use a coke forge when demonstrating forging techniques because it means that the steel can be brought up to heat more quickly. The high working temperatures that can be achieved with coke or other solid fuels, however, can also bring problems. The centre of a coke forge reaches a temperature of about 2,200° Celsius and, since most of the steel used for making knife blades burns at around 1,450°C, you have to be very careful when working thin steel in a solid-fuel forge. If your attention wanders or you do not keep moving the steel around, you will inevitably burn your steel.

You can tell if the steel has burned because the material will spark like a sparkler. When using modern carbon steel this can be a fatal mistake, since it is very risky to incorporate burned steel into a finished knife blade.

When you heat up a piece of carbon steel, it first becomes red hot and then turns orange. I like to do most of my forging at an orange heat and stop before the steel cools in air to red. As the steel continues to heat up into bright orange and then yellow, the surface starts to look slightly slick, as if it is covered in hot honey. This indicates that the surface is melting and at this point the steel will start to spark. Sparks are a definite indication that the steel is burning, but by then it is already too late just to pull the steel from the fire since they show that the carbon steel is ruined.

If the steel being used to forge a knife has been burned it should be considered as ruined. Remove the whole burnt area and a little more to make sure burnt steel has not been incorporated into a finished piece. In practice this often means starting afresh with a new piece of steel.

If you have some experience forging with mild steel or wrought iron it is worth remembering that carbon steel and

When steel burns it's like a sparkler.

mild steel behave quite differently at high temperature. Mild steel is a lot more forgiving than carbon steel. You can often get away with burning mild steel or wrought iron as they will hammer weld (forge weld) back together quite happily without any real detriment to their structure. This is not the case with carbon steel. When it is brought near burning temperature it undergoes changes that have a detrimental effect on its structure, since the loss of some of its carbon as it burns will affect the steel's hardenability and how it performs as a blade.

An even more important factor is that as carbon steel overheats its grain becomes more pronounced. This is known as blown grain. As the steel nears its burning point, this happens to such an extent that oxygen from the fire starts to combine with the steel. As the temperature increases it can oxidise the grain boundaries of the steel. This oxidation turns the steel to something resembling mushy yellow hot cottage cheese. (For more information about grain growth, *see* Chapter 5.) If you were to hammer weld the steel back together at this temperature it would most likely weld up, provided you did it correctly, but you would still have oxygen ingress at the grain boundaries of the steel. This means you would be forging oxidised steel into your blade with the almost inevitable result that at some point this internal oxidation would cause the blade to crack.

It is far safer to assume that if carbon steel is heated to the point of burning it is ruined, especially when making something such as a knife, which relies so much on the integrity of the materials from which it is made.

It is worth remembering that solid-fuel forges can be very oxidising in front of the air blast or tue-iron.

A solid-fuel fire is split into three zones. The area in front of the air blast is marked by an excess of oxygen from the air coming into the forge. Since this area is very oxidising it is also the hottest part of the forge, so you should avoid digging the blade into this area of the fire or you will most certainly burn it.

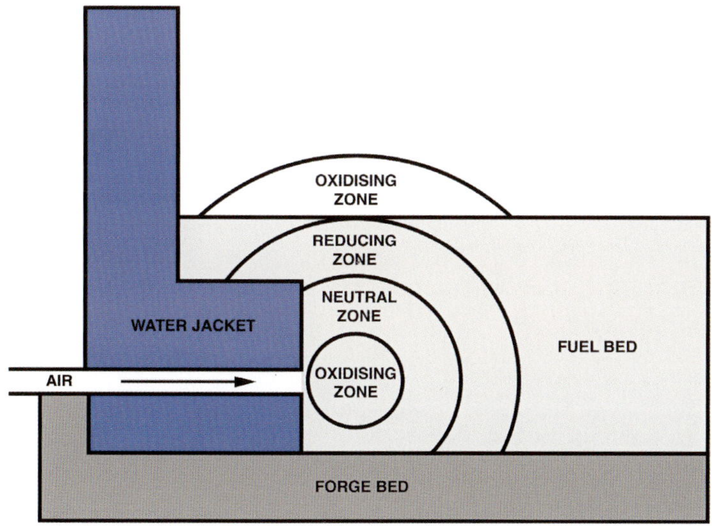

The temperature within a solid-fuel forge varies depending on the proportion of air being burned by the fuel.

If possible the blade should be placed in the fire just under the coals.

Around the oxidising area is a neutral zone, where the incoming air is equal to the burning fuel. Around the neutral zone is a reducing zone where the hot fuel does not get enough air to burn completely. Above the reducing zone there is another oxidising zone where the burning fuel mixes with the air surrounding the forge.

If possible the steel should always be placed in the neutral or reducing zones of the fire. In practice this means having the steel just under the surface of the burning fuel and constantly making sure that you are rotating the steel to get it evenly hot.

You really can't leave a knife blade in a coke forge for any length of time. Instead you have to pay full attention to the temperature of the steel and the fire as long as the blade is in the fire.

Coal

Regulations concerning smoke-free zones mean that the option of burning coal is out of the question in many areas due to the large amount of acrid smoke it produces. Many smiths who live in areas where these regulations do not apply, however, choose to use it. If you find yourself in a similar situation it may be a suitable fuel for your needs. Make sure that a smithing coal is chosen that it is very low in sulphur. Some coal burns very brightly and its bright white glare can temporarily blind you, so be careful not to look at the fire for too long when burning coal. You will often get a much better idea about the temperature of the steel by quickly removing it from the fire and looking at it in ambient light.

Unlike coke, which goes out when the air blast is stopped, coal (and charcoal) will keep on burning when the forge's air blast is turned off, so make sure the coal is extinguished when you have finished forging. It is also a good idea to keep a long-handled water sprinkler at hand when forging with coal in order to dampen down the area around the fire and keep its size in check. One of the great things about coal as a fuel is that it cokes down as it burns and sticks to itself. This makes it possible to create a wonderful hollow cave with burning walls that radiate heat into the 'cave'.

Charcoal

I occasionally use a charcoal forge or mix some of this with the coke. Most of the knives that have ever been made were forged on a charcoal forge, as it was the smithing fuel used from the Iron Age all the way until the Industrial Revolution. Charcoal burns at quite a high temperature, but it is not a dense fuel and it can be hard to achieve a good hot fire. When using charcoal I tend to build a little brick trough in my forge to contain some of the heat. Charcoal produces quite a soft fire and I like it as a fuel, but you should be aware that the sparks given off by charcoal like fireflies can cause a nasty burn. Charcoal produces a lot of ash in the bed of the fire and it is necessary to keep on top of this by raking out the burned charcoal ash or the fire will become blocked up.

Charcoal can be added to coke to vary the quality of the flame.

Gas forges

Most of my forging work is carried out in a gas forge. I was initially taught on coke and coal forges, but as the years have passed my coke forge forging has been reduced to forging demonstrations and the rare occasion when I am unable to get a strangely shaped object into the gas forge.

Unlike a solid-fuel forge, a gas forge does not get too hot and it is possible to set it to a temperature well below the burning point of steel. Most of my gas forges at Bushfire Forge run at temperatures of about 1,250 to 1,300°C, although I also have hot gas forges that run in excess of 1,400°C for when making Damascus steel.

Gas forges come in many different types, including both naturally aspirated designs, with a venturi device pulling air into the burner, or blown air types, with the air supplied by an electric blower. I use gas forges that I have made as well as ones that I have purchased.

A well-used gas Swan Portaforge.

When using a gas forge a temperature can be maintained so that the steel does not burn.

One of the author's homemade forges.

Gas forges also produce combustion gases, so it is important that the forge area is well ventilated. In fact I would say that when working with gas this is even more important than with coal and coke forges. Carbon monoxide is a particular problem with gas forges that are running rich (that is, they have more fuel than air in their mix). Although this often provides an ideal setting for heating steel as it reduces oxidation, extra care has to be taken to make sure that a gas forge is ventilated. The exhaust fumes from a gas forge are not visible, unlike coal smoke, and the carbon monoxide produced is both invisible and odour free. Always install a CO monitor when using a gas forge and make sure the area is well ventilated. Carbon monoxide is known as the 'silent killer' and requires serious consideration: my gas forges have been set up under cover outside the building and not inside.

The disadvantage of a gas forge is that it takes longer for the steel to heat up. In order not to waste time I normally work on two pieces of steel in the forge together. This is a much less risky proposition when using a gas forge than it would be in a coke forge, where you could find yourself juggling the pieces of steel to stop them burning by literally having too many irons in the fire.

The secret to using a gas forge is to forge hot and fast. Since the steel will only heat up to the maximum temperature of the forge, you can allow it to reach the same temperature as the forge. This is evident when the steel is the same orange colour as the forge lining. The orange steel can then be worked at the anvil for a short time before being put back in the gas forge while the steel is still orange.

Thermocouple

A thermocouple is a really useful tool that gives a spot temperature reading in the forge. This makes it very handy for checking the temperature when heat-treating or helping to confirm your visual judgement of the temperature in the gas forge. The most common type of these digital thermometers is the type K thermocouple, which is reliable and can be bought cheaply online.

When steel is ready for working it will be the same colour as the lining of the forge.

The probe connected to this type K thermocouple gives an instant reading of the forge's temperature.

HAMMERS AND ANVILS

The basic tools of every blacksmith and bladesmith are the hammer and anvil, although the techniques with which they are employed in each craft can differ a little. If you are coming at bladesmithing from a background as a blacksmith, there are a few things that you may need to alter in your set-up.

Anvils

Most of the forging that a bladesmith performs is done on a very small area of the anvil, about 15 square centimetres on the section of the anvil face next to the projecting bick or beak. As a result there is really no need for a traditional London pattern anvil. If you are looking for an anvil it is worth remembering that you may be able to get away with a large block of steel instead of an expensive anvil. That being said, an anvil is a wonderful tool, it has unparalleled longevity and provides a great focal centre for a forge. Anvil prices in the UK have increased in recent years, but it is still possible to find second-hand examples online, although I would advise examining an anvil in person before purchasing it. Look for signs of severe wear, delamination and nicks and gouges. I would not buy a heavily painted anvil as this can often disguise a flaw of some kind.

There are two main construction methods for anvils. The older traditional anvils are made by forge welding a wrought iron body made up from multiple pieces to a steel face; more modern anvils are cast steel. Both types of anvil are quite usable, although I have a fondness for the older wrought anvils as they are such a strong piece of our working heritage.

There are several types of anvil suitable for bladesmithing:

London pattern anvil. The typical traditional tool of the blacksmith: look for one with a step between the anvil face and the bick.

Portsmouth or dockyard anvil. These double-bicked anvils are much sought after and are really useful for making sockets and forging the insides of eyes on axes.

The basic tools of every bladesmith are their hammer and an anvil.

London pattern anvil.

Portsmouth pattern anvil.

Sheffield toolmaker's anvil.

Bladesmith's anvil.

Saw doctor's anvil. Blocky flat anvils of this type with four usable corners are very useful for bladesmithing. In the UK they are often much cheaper than the standard London pattern anvil.

Bladesmith's stump anvil. Because of the small area used for the majority of bladesmithing, a stump anvil can be a perfect alternative to a full-sized anvil. The important thing is to have a lot of weight under the face, so a piece of hydraulic piston rod or large machine spindle can make a great stump anvil. Stump anvils are now available that are both economic to buy and easy to move around, while also giving a really good forging surface and great usable shaped formers. I use these anvils in my knifemaking school.

Traditional Sheffield bladesmith's anvil. The traditional Sheffield bladesmith's anvil is now somewhat of a rarity in the UK, although the European variants are widely available in Europe. These are industrial anvils with replaceable pallets that can be changed over from one job to the next and replaced when worn out, which can happen to even an anvil – eventually. My current forging anvil for teaching is one of this type.

Judging the correct height of the anvil by the position of your knuckles when standing next to it.

Mounting your anvil

For the purposes of bladesmithing I mount my anvils a little higher than I would as a general blacksmithing anvil. The forging done when bladesmithing requires much more repetitive hammer flattening than the scrolling and bending done by a decorative smith. Because of this I mount my bladesmithing anvils a good 5 to 10 centimetres higher than the prescribed height for a blacksmithing anvil, which is recommended as being at the height of one's knuckles when you stand by the anvil with your fist held down by your side.

As always there will be an element of personal taste when judging anvil height. I mount my anvils on wooden stands, with spacers to adjust the anvil height for students. Metal stands or a good solid stump, the traditional way to mount an anvil, both work well. It is important that the anvil is prevented from walking off its stand as it is being forged on. In order to hold the anvil in place I screw lengths of 47 × 22mm timber around it.

Before forging it is worth checking the anvil for any cracking or mushrooming around the edges. This should be removed and then dressed in with an angle grinder. I have noticed that this can particularly be a problem with cast steel anvils such as those made by Brooks.

Posture at the anvil is important, as is the way that you hold and swing your hammer. When they first try to work hot metal on an anvil, many people hold their body a long way from the anvil as they are a little afraid of the hot steel and the hammer blows. This practice puts you at an immediate disadvantage as you are having to lift the hammer at a long lever disadvantage to your body, which makes the work of forging a lot harder. It also makes it harder to place the steel correctly where you want it on the anvil.

Instead you should work closer to the anvil, striking the hammer blows with your arms bent and holding the steel closer to your body.

Holding your body too far away from the anvil is both uncomfortable and inefficient.

Good posture for accurate bladesmithing.

Hammers

There is much debate about the correct way to hold and use a hammer, but I would take all of this controversy with a pinch of salt. Many people hold fixed but conflicting opinions about what is right and what is not. I have tried to avoid fixed ideas as my own technique and style have evolved the more I learn.

There are, however, some universal threads that run through the various opinions on the best ways to swing a hammer. I also observe some personal rules that I use when trying to avoid fatigue from hammering.

Choose a hammer that is not too heavy for you. This will, of course, depend on your strength and how accustomed you are to using hand tools. For most bladesmithing I forge with hammers ranging between 2 and 3 pounds (0.9–1.4kg). Working with a hammer that is too heavy for you is a certain way to injure yourself.

Selection of bladesmithing hammers.

I have generally observed that good smiths do not look as though they are hitting the steel all that hard, but rather that the steel appears to be moving under their soft blows.

You should always try to hold the hammer lightly in your hand, as if you are guiding the blows rather than gripping the hammer in a death grip. This will allow some of the energy from the hammer impacting the metal to travel back as the initial lift when the hammer rebounds. That way you get the first few centimetres of lift for free. A light grip will also transfer less of the jarring impact back up your arms.

Many beginners have a tendency to try and push the hammer into the work, hitting and then pressing the hammer down after impact. With the best will in the world it is not possible to move hot steel by pressing it with the hammer. All that you are achieving is to prevent any rebound generated by the hammer from helping you lift the hammer before the next blow.

Try to keep your wrist movement fairly fixed while hammering. This allows the movement to happen at the elbow and shoulder, since our wrists are fairly weak compared to our biceps and shoulder muscles.

It is worth remembering that gravity is your friend when it comes to hammering. If you want to hit the metal harder, lift the hammer higher. The force exerted upon the metal is a direct product of the hammer's velocity and its weight. The weight is fixed, so if you want more force from your strikes it is better to lift the hammer higher and then allow gravity to aid the hammer's acceleration downwards. It is worth noting that, counter-intuitively, this means you have to slow down your hammering in order to hit harder with the hammer.

I like to think of hammering as a slow race: there is no prize for coming first. Rather the idea is to work at a pace that you can maintain for as long as possible. In my case I pace

Lifting height for light hammering.

Lifting height for heavy hammering.

myself to make sure I may still be forging in ten or fifteen years' time!

It is generally considered bad form to hold a hammer with your thumb on the back of the handle as this can jar some of the forearm tendons and lead to nerve damage. I must note that, while I was taught this at college and pass on the information as best practice, I have observed some wonderful smiths still working into their seventies who either ignored this advice or had never heard of it, happily forging away thumb on hammer.

As mentioned earlier, there are no firm rules for correct injury-free hammering, so it is up to you to judge your pace and style of hammering and find a way that works for you.

Whenever possible I try to avoid using tongs when I am bladesmithing. I prefer to directly handle the bar I am forging in my gloved hand and find that I get a much better feel for the subtleties of the work that way, especially when forging bevels. I would recommend not wearing a glove on your hammer hand, as the glove will certainly reduce the control you get from touching the hammer's handle with the bare hand.

Whereas some smiths only ever seem to use one hammer, I have a lot of different hammers I like to use for forging a blade. I must admit to a love of blacksmithing tools. Although I make my own forging hammers, I love to acquire and use as many old hammers as I can. I guess it's a bit like wearing your dad's jumper: for me these tools have taken on a life of their own and I really enjoy imagining the steel and iron that may have passed under the face of an old hammer.

For the exacting job of forging bevels I like to use a weight-forward or dog's head hammer, in which most of the weight is positioned forward of the handle. The head is often slanted slightly downward from the hammer.

Hammers like these have been almost universal throughout history in industrial smithing situations where a hammer is needed for giving repetitive blows. I find them harder hitting and more accurate than a general-purpose hammer. I also like the idea of using the same kind of tooling as the Viking smiths I admire so much, as well as their modern counterparts, the Japanese bladesmiths, cutlers, saw doctors and file makers.

Holding your thumb on the back of the hammer is not recommended, but many experienced bladesmiths work this way.

Holding my favourite bladesmithing hammer.

OTHER TOOLS

Tongs

Although I try to avoid using tongs when bladesmithing, it often becomes an inevitable part of the smithing process. Sometimes I will weld a temporary handle onto the end of a sword tang in order to have a fixed handle on the sword. On occasion, however, I find myself using tongs, which are very useful to have around the forge and essential when handling small items such as sword guards.

Vice

You will probably end up with many vices, which are useful for holding work when you are filing, using rotary tools or grinding.

Bladesmithing tongs.

Leg vice.

Grinders

Belt grinder

The belt grinder is in some ways a bladesmith's most important tool. A blade may be born in the fire but it is brought to completion on the belt grinder. Belt grinders are expensive but they are worth every penny.

The rise in popularity of knifemaking has meant that quite a few purpose-built knife-making grinders are now available. One rule of thumb is that a belt grinder should produce 1hp for every 2.5cm of belt width for it to be usable on metal. Basic single-speed grinders are available, but I would advise saving up for a grinder with variable speed. Preferably this should be fitted with an inverter controller rather than one on which it is necessary to change pulleys in order to

Bladesmith's belt grinder.

Belt grinder fitted with multiple contact wheels.

change its speed. A variable-speed grinder is such a versatile workshop tool and can happily do fine finishing as well as hogging steel.

Angle grinder

I have many of these amazing tools, which are great for cutting steel and grinding profiles that are hard to reach. I would certainly recommend at least one grinder for any workshop, together with a selection of grinding, cutting and sanding discs.

Dremels and pendant grinders

Dremels and pendant grinders are great tools for fine work. Many burrs, discs and grinding attachments are available for various tasks. They are very versatile tools and I increasingly find new uses for which they are helpful.

115mm angle grinder.

Many different attachments are available for use with Dremel multitools.

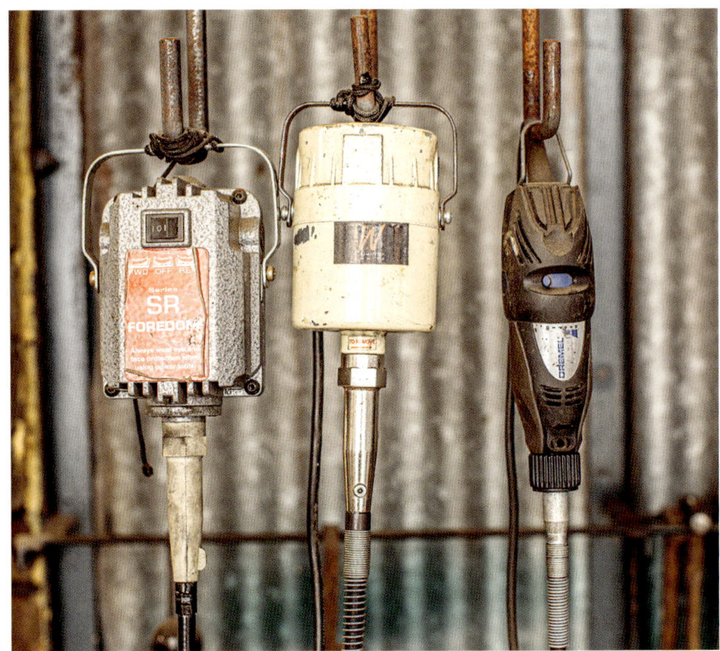

Rotary tools by (from left to right) Fordham, Axminster and Dremel.

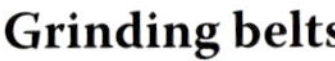

Grinding belts

Grinding belts are the workface of the grinder. They come in a confusing array of materials and prices. It's up to you to choose a range of belts that fits your grinding requirements and budget. The choice of abrasive belt types available in the UK has greatly increased in recent years. It is worth trying some of the many finishing belts available as they will certainly speed up the finishing process.

Aluminium oxide is the basic grinding belt and does a good job of removing steel. I tend to use these belts as finishing belts.

Ceramic belts last much longer than aluminium oxide belts. These belts are used mainly for hogging steel as they remove steel at a faster rate.

Shaped ceramic belts are the bee's knees of grinding belts. The shaped ceramic particles break down to sharper shaped grit and have the fastest material removal rate. They are amazing belts, but they are also very expensive, so you have to decide whether they are right for the way you work.

I work with ceramic belts up to 120 grit and then finish the job with aluminium oxide. Once belts start to get dull I tend to throw them away as my need for speed is more important than getting the best value from the belts. With grinding you get what you pay for: better belts are more expensive and cheaper belts do not get as much work done.

Belt grits

I do most of my grinding with coarse grits, either 24 or 36 grit, and consider all of the other grades as finishing grits. Since it takes a powerful grinder to make the most of 24 grit belts and a lot of force is needed, many people prefer 36 grit. I am a greedy grinder, however, and love how 24 grit blasts material away. My standard progression is to grind material to size with 24 or 36 grit and then finish with 60, 120, 240 and 400 grit. I then go on to hand sanding from 400 grit and upwards.

Grinder fitted with a coarse grit belt.

Aluminium oxide belt used for finishing.

Hand sanding

Sanding blades by hand is a way to refine the finish achieved on the belt grinder. I always have a stock of sandpaper in 120, 240, 400 and 800 grit. Buy the best-quality hand-sanding abrasive you can find. There is no economy in cheap abrasive paper. When cleaning up blades I wrap the hand-sanding paper around a wooden block.

When sanding by hand the sandpaper should be wrapped around a wooden block.

Bench hand tools

Bladesmiths find that they will acquire a wide variety of hand tools, including files of assorted sizes, hand vices, chisels and craft knives.

Heat-treating oven

Although blades can be heat treated in a simple fashion in a forge, as soon as you get serious about knife-making some kind of heat-treatment oven will be needed. You will find that having control of the temperatures at which blades are normalised, hardened and tempered will make the results much more consistent. A heat-treating oven then becomes a necessity rather than a luxury when you are using some of the more complex carbon steels. This also applies to stainless steel.

Bench tools to keep to hand include files, nippers, a craft knife and pliers.

Heat-treating oven.

Quenching oil

Quenching oil is an important tool in the bladesmith's toolbox. Although you can get away with quenching most modern steels at blade section thickness using canola (rapeseed) oil, this is not really optimal. A commercial heat-treating oil will give better and more consistent results for a much longer time. I use five different commercial quenching oils with different quench speeds and recommend the varieties made by Exol Lubricants and those derived from the formulation of Parks 50:

- Exelquench 601 standard rate industrial quench oil
- Exelquench L603Z fast quench oil (although nowhere near as fast as Parks 50)
- Exelquench L1664Z marquenching oil for hot quenching
- Parks 50 fast quench oil for low hardenable steels

Once again a much wider choice of oils is available in the UK compared to a few years ago, including a number of clones of the US-made 50 Parks.

The various types of quenching oil have different properties, so you may need more than one.

PERSONAL PROTECTION EQUIPMENT (PPE)

Without doubt the most important tool in a bladesmith's toolbox is the respirator.

I wear a powered respirator whenever grinding or exposing myself to any dust or vapour, including oil vapour. It is essential to have at least a decent FFP2 or FFP3 mask. The half masks made by 3M are an industry standard. Powered respirators are expensive but make life more pleasant as well as being safer.

I use a 3M Adflo powered air purifying respirator mask and highly recommend them. They are expensive, however, and there are now equivalent models made by other welding mask manufacturers. Those made by ESAB have been recommended by friends.

Safety glasses are another must as they should be worn at all times when working. Remember that if you are working around other people it's not just you who can cause sparks or create dangerous dust.

A leather apron is great for saving your clothes and skin from getting burned.

Workshop clothes need to be non-flammable. The canvas workshop trousers made by Carhartt are double fronted and amazingly hard wearing.

As you will be standing for hours on end when making knives, money spent on comfortable leather workshop boots is well spent.

Leather gloves are very useful when working hot metal. When working with glue, however, or for ensuring you don't get fingerprints on your blades, you should always use disposable nitrile gloves

PPE essentials: leather apron and gloves, eye protection and an FFP2 mask.

A 3M Adflo powered air purifying respirator mask is expensive but a worthwhile purchase.

Never skimp on the quality of your PPE.

ADVANCED TOOLS OF THE TRADE

Power hammer

Power hammers are the most amazing tools. Using a power hammer is like being a superhero. A power hammer or press is one of the fundamental tools for a professional bladesmith and it allows you to work at a pace you can only dream about when working by hand.

I have run and owned many power hammers, both mechanical and air hammers. Both types have their own advantages. Mechanical hammers, for example, are cheaper to purchase and cheaper to run. Air hammers, however, offer more versatility and are better when using with handheld tools as they have a fixed stroke rate. I now do most of my work on a two-hundredweight Alldays & Onions power hammer made during World War II.

Finding a power hammer can be a challenge as second-hand hammers often sell very quickly when offered for sale online. There are now, however, some really very good new power hammers for sale. Chinese-made Anyang hammers are top quality and are offered for sale in the UK by Massey Forging. I would highly recommend their forging tools.

Hydraulic power press

The homemade hydraulic press I have used for quite a while has been an amazing tool. I recently changed up to a new Anyang hydraulic press and it has changed my way of working completely. They can transform the work possible in a smith's

A 2cwt Alldays & Onions power hammer.

Anyang 50-ton hydraulic forging press.

workshop, especially when making Damascus steel. The power and ease of use of one of these presses is unbelievable.

If asked which is the better tool for the smith – a power hammer or a hydraulic press – I say that both deserve their place. A power hammer is more versatile and better suited for the thin material that a bladesmith uses, but the hydraulic press's action is easier on the body and the way it forges large section hot steel has to be seen to be believed.

Surface grinder

I have found that a surface grinder has an innovative effect on my work. I have converted a couple to work with contact wheels and abrasive belts. They are incredible workhorses that will hog material in a ceaseless and very meticulous way. These are the only machines I use that can get a long working life from an abrasive belt as they can provide the necessary feed rate to get the most from the belts. They are huge machines, though, and are really limited to the serious professional.

Rolling mill

A rolling mill is the ultimate tool for making hot steel thinner and longer. This means it is essential if you are serious about laminating or making Damascus steel. That said, they are truly dangerous tools and really only suited for professionals who understand how dangerous they are.

McDonald rolling mill

This really useful tool is a home-workshop version of the rolling mill designed by the Australian engineer Hugh McDonald. It has jaws that open and shut using your weight on a foot pedal at a large (about 60:1) lever advantage. The great thing about these mills is that they feed material back towards the operator and are therefore so much safer to use than a fixed-gap rolling mill, which can pull you into the machine. The way in which you apply your weight to the foot pedal means you can draw tapers on these machines. Mills to McDonald's design are available for sale or plans can be found to make your own.

Surface grinder.

Hille 25 rolling mill.

Plans are available to make your own McDonald rolling mill.

CHAPTER 2

THE BLADESMITH'S MATERIALS

FERROUS METALS

Steel

Steel is the basic material of the bladesmith. There are so many steels available to the modern smith that it can be confusing when trying to choose one to use for making a knife. It is easy to get caught up in the hype associated with modern steels, but it is worth remembering that simple carbon steels have been used for making blades for two or three millennia.

Modern knifemaking has led to the development of many new steels, some of which have amazing properties. Normally, however, there are often shortcomings involved in the material. Ultra-hard high carbon steels are sold as performance steels. They get very hard and will hold an edge well, but in my experience they are very chippy and brittle and hard to sharpen, which is why I prefer to use a simpler carbon steel. Most of the blades I have made have been made from 1080-type steels (steels with around 0.75–0.85 percent carbon), which fall into the middle ground of steels. They do their job very well, are easy to work with and sharpen, take a great edge and hold it well. They are also tough and flexible if heat treated appropriately for their intended use.

Like so many other aspects of making knives, steel choice is a compromise. When you choose steel do not be dazzled by one of its attributes, try to look at the whole picture. The chosen steel must be appropriate for your method of making and tools as well as for its final use. There is no 'ultimate steel.' You are often better off learning to use, master and then understand one type of steel rather than chasing the new trendy ultra-steel.

The preferred steel for most of the monosteel knives I make is En42j and this is the variety used within this book, although I do use many other types when making Damascus steel or for use making tools.

Alongside the increasing interest in knifemaking in the UK in recent years, it is now much easier to acquire steels than it was when I started out making knives.

It is worth remembering that steel can be bought in many different forms and quantities. I get most of my steel in bulk in sheet form and use an electric guillotine to cut it to size.

When buying in smaller quantities, however, the relative price goes up. Before buying any material it is worth calculating the price per kilogram, which will enable you to compare the value of one steel with another. Among the most commonly available steel varieties are:

The bladesmith may choose to use many types of ferrous and non-ferrous metals as well as organic materials such as wood and horn.

Different sections of carbon steel.

En42J	
Carbon	0.75–0.8%
Manganese	0.35–0.5%

En42J is a 0.8 percent carbon steel designed for making large band-saw blades and springs. It is the steel I use most for knife making. Available as plate, it makes a very good general-use knife.

CS80	
Carbon	0.75–0.8%
Manganese	0.35–0.5%

CS80 is the thinner sheet steel designation of EN24J and normally comes in a hardened and tempered state. I use it for the Damascus steel I make as its manganese content is slightly different to my usual EN42J and etches slightly darker.

15N20	
Carbon	0.75%
Nickel	2.0%
Manganese	0.4%

15N20 is a premium band saw steel with a 2 percent nickel content. This makes the steel very tough and resistant to etching. I use it as the bright steel when making Damascus steel. It also makes for a good tough knife.

En8	
Carbon	0.35–0.45%
Manganese	0.6–1.0%

En8 is a medium carbon steel with around 0.4 percent carbon content. I use it for making hammers. It is also a good choice for guards and bolsters as it is tough and takes a much better polish than mild steel.

En9	
Carbon	0.5–0.6%
Silicon	0.4%
Manganese	0.5–0.8%

En9 is a general-use medium carbon steel. I use it for making blacksmiths' tools, such as punches, chisels and drifts. It also makes a great steel for axes, since it has better edge-holding properties than En8. It is very forgiving in heat treatment and is an acceptable choice for making knives.

En45	
Carbon	0.55–0.6%
Manganese	0.7–1.0%
Silicon	1.5–2.0%

En45 is a premium silicone spring steel that is tough as old boots. I use it for monosteel sword blades and really love it. It is, however, not really suitable for a beginner as the heat treatment requires an austenitising temperature of 900°C and there is really no way to get that accurately without a heat-treating oven. It has a bad reputation for this reason and I think that many blades made with this steel have not been properly heat treated.

Stainless steel

I do not work much in stainless steel as I have found that I prefer the traditional aesthetic and sharpening characteristics of carbon steel. There is no doubting that stainless steel is in many ways a wonderful material, especially some of the modern martensitic powder metallurgy stainless steels with a high chromium content. The lack of upkeep needed when using stainless steel makes them a practical choice for the casual user, but I have yet to find a place within my own work (or heart) for this amazing material.

Martensitic stainless steel

Martensitic stainless steels can be hardened and they are less stain resistant than the austenitic stainless steels. For the bladesmith stainless steel has some heat-treatment requirements and working attributes that take them out of the range of the beginner, but you may find that they fit into your way of working and aesthetic.

Stainless steel.

Austenitic stainless steel

These are the standard stainless steel varieties that you will encounter used for such as high-class hand rails and fixtures. The large amount of chrome in this steel means that under normal circumstances they really don't rust. The generally available austenitic 316 and 304 stainless steels make great fittings for knives, but they are hard to work and are tough on tools, requiring a lot of force to forge.

Pattern-welded or Damascus steel

There is no hiding the fact that I love Damascus steel. I still find the act of creating and working with this material to be one of the real pleasures of the craft. I experience the same thrill when I reveal etch a piece of simple randomly patterned Damascus as I did when I made my first piece nearly three

Damascus steel is also known as pattern-welded steel.

decades ago. We will not go into the making of Damascus steel here as it is really deserves its own book, but the material is available to purchase and use and I would recommend trying it as it is a wonderful material to make knives from.

Wrought iron

Wrought iron is the traditional form of iron that was made throughout history until it was overtaken in the twentieth century. It has a stringy granular nature with silicate layers running through it. These stringers are formed as the material is forged from a slag-infused bloom of iron. Wrought iron is in many ways a very inferior material to the mild steel that replaced it. It can be a beautiful material, however, if it is etched. Wrought iron is much loved by blacksmiths because it is very easy to forge weld at a high heat, when the silicates melt and the wrought iron becomes self fluxing. It is also very stable at high temperatures.

Laminated steel

In some ways laminated steel, also known as San Mai (three-layer steel), offers the best of both worlds as it combines features making it suitable for edge steel and a cladding material. These laminated materials allow a very hard carbon steel core with a much softer cladding. The many varieties of laminated steel available range from simple laminates of mild steel with a carbon steel core to stainless steel with a carbon steel core. There are even more exotic laminated materials with copper and brass in the mix. These steels are well worth exploring.

Mild steel

Mild steel is the basic structural steel used by fabricators and blacksmiths. It is not hardenable, however, so is of no use for knife blades, but it is useful for making items for the workshop or bolsters on knives.

Wrought iron.

Laminated San Mai (three-layer steel) has a carbon steel core with stainless steel cladding.

Mild steel.

NON-FERROUS METALS

Brass, copper and bronze are all materials that I use in the workshop for making knife fittings, sword fittings and scabbard and sheath parts. They are all wonderful materials to work with.

In order to bring an element of wonder and bling to a knife-making project there is nothing to equal decoration in silver and gold.

Copper and brass are among the non-ferrous metals that can be used.

Gold, silver and jewels can be applied as period decoration.

ORGANIC MATERIALS

A vast array of types of wood is available for the knife maker to choose from. I tend to stick with varieties that are native to Europe, however, as it fits the aesthetic of the knives I make. Wood is often available ready cut into knife handle blanks, which are very convenient for the knife maker, although it is much more economical to buy the wood in larger quantities.

Many of the knives I make incorporate horn and bone. These are natural materials that complement the texture of the steel and there is an ancient tradition of their use in knife making.

Wood can be purchased in its natural state or as pre-cut blocks for handles.

Horn and bone can also come ready-sliced.

UKS

CHAPTER 3

FORGING THE BLADE

Forging is the basic process of the bladesmith; the blade is shaped by hammer and anvil into a knife blank where it is ready to grind.

THE BASICS OF FORGING

I now do all of my forging using a gas forge, since I find it has obvious advantages over a traditional coal or charcoal forge. The principal of these is that you can control the temperature of the forge and set it well below the burning temperature of the steel. A coal or coke forge has a core temperature of about 2,200°C and most of the carbon steel we use melts or burns at around 1,500°C. I usually have my gas forges set around 1,200 to 1,250°C.

What we are trying to do when forging is to heat the steel, which is very hard at room temperature, until it becomes soft enough to be deformed using a hammer over an anvil.

It is possible to judge the temperature of the heated steel by its colour, which should be the same as that of the lining of the gas forge. It is really important to get the steel as hot as

Heating the blade in a gas forge.

Forging a knife blank at the anvil.

the forge will allow, as it becomes a lot harder to forge when it cools down.

The steel should be forged for a short while and then returned to the fire while it is still at an orange colour. This way the steel will heat up quickly to the temperature of the forge and allow you to return to the forging sooner.

It is tempting and quite natural to concentrate on the hammering aspect of the forging as that's where the work is done. You will get more work done for a given time or for a given amount of effort, however, if you work while your material is hot. If you get carried away with the forging, you may find that the steel cools down to red or dull orange before it is put back into the forge. To avoid this I start counting my hammer blows, giving twelve to fifteen blows before putting the steel back into the forge while it is still glowing orange.

Before you start forging a blade it is worth considering exactly what result you want to achieve. Ideally this should be a forged blade that is bigger in every dimension than the final blade you have in mind, together with the forged-in bevels that you can feel and reference when the blade is taken to the grinder. At this stage the blade should be a little wider and longer than the finished knife. It should also be quite a bit thicker, a minimum of 1.5mm at least at the edge and thicker at the spine. At least 0.5mm will be ground away off each face of the blade when it is taken to the grinder.

I break my forging into three separate stages: forging the tang; forging a preform shape; and forging the blade bevels.

The colour shows that the blade is at temperature in the gas forge.

Three stages of making a blade (from top to bottom): a preform blade; a blade forged with bevels; a blade with outline ground.

FORGING THE TANG

Depending on the size of the stock being used, there are two very different ways of starting to forge a blade. If forging a blade from bar stock I tend to start at the tip of the blade and forge back from there. The rest of the bar becomes the handle and as much work as possible is done on the blade while the blade is still attached to its bar.

When forging from a smaller billet, however, I normally start by forging the blade's tang (the part of the blade that goes into the handle). The reason for forging the tang first is that it provides some part of the blade that is easy to hold: a stubby tang can be easily gripped and manipulated by a pair of round- or square-jawed tongs. As you will find, using tongs to hold the steel can be the most complicated part of forging a knife.

Depending on the width of the blade being forged there are two ways to forge a tang. On material 2.5cm wide or less the tang is forged over the edge of the anvil. For material of any greater width the tang is forged over a modified cut-off hardy. A hardy is basically an upside-down chisel that fits in a square hole on the anvil, known as the hardy hole. If a small section of the hardy's blade has been blunted, this section can be used to forge a small radius between the tang and the blade.

Most of the knives I make have stick tangs. Sometimes these go all the way through the handle of the knife, while others have a hidden tang that goes some 6 or 7cm into the handle.

Start by cutting a blank blade billet. This normally has a 45-degree angle cut at one end in order to make it easier to forge the blade tip.

Forging the tang.

One end of the billet is cut at 45 degrees.

Monkey-tail tongs (right) and bladesmith's tongs.

Marking the hot steel with soapstone.

Sharply striking the soapstone line on the edge of the anvil results in a dent to mark the start of the tang.

The correct way of forging the tang indent.

Monkey-tail or bladesmith's tongs are used to hold the billet while the tang is being forged. Once the tang has been forged it is much easier to hold the blade by the tang with round-jawed tongs.

When forging a tang on the edge of the anvil, heat the steel and then mark a 2cm line on the hot steel using engineer's chalk (soapstone). I usually mark the anvil first and then use the soapstone to transfer the line from the anvil to the hot steel. In this way there is no risk of a ruler or tape measure getting burned by the hot steel.

Take the steel immediately to a sharp corner of the anvil and, holding the steel at 45 degrees from vertical, give it a sharp hit on the anvil. This results in a small dent that can be used as a reference when forging the tang.

A bigger dent is then forged into the steel over a rounded corner of the anvil, making sure the hammer blows are placed so that they force the steel around the corner of the anvil. This is done by aiming as though trying to hit the corner of the anvil through the steel.

If the material is hit too high or too low the bar will be bent and it will need to be straightened (*see* below).

As the steel is being forged it thickens up. This means it is necessary to place the steel flat on the anvil and hammer the thickness back to its original size. This is one of the unavoidable features of forging. At every stage of the process the bladesmith is constantly forging corrections. An example might be when a dent has to be made in the steel to separate out the tang, but the steel thickens when it is hammered so it must be forged back. This process of two steps forward and one step back is the dance of the bladesmith. The corrections are important and must be carried out every heat or every other heat.

Forge the steel over the edge of the anvil until there is a dent halfway through the width of the steel. It is important that you do not forge the steel thinner than this. The junction between the tang and the blade is the most important part of the knife as this is where it is most likely to fail due to the big difference in the cross-section at this point. Once the tang has

Forging the tang incorrectly with the hammer over the anvil.

Forging the tang incorrectly with the hammer over the blade.

been separated from the blade it is time to go about forging the shape of the tang.

It is important to keep the blade section of the steel clear of the face of the anvil while forging the tang. This will keep it from being damaged or malformed when the tang is forged to shape.

Forge the tang so that it tapers in both width and thickness. The tang should be widest where it meets the blade and the same thickness as the blade steel where it meets the blade. It then tapers back from that in both dimensions. Remember that the anvil as well as the hammer forge the shape of the steel, so the angle at which the steel is held against the anvil will have as much effect as the angle it is struck by the hammer. At this stage you are not trying to forge a finished tang but a thick and strong proto-tang that can easily be held in round-jaw tongs.

Rounding the intersection of the tang to the blade.

When the blade thickens it should be forged over the edge of the anvil.

Forging the finished tang.

A hardy tool is required when separating the tang from the broader blade of chef's knives, which have a large blade transition.

The sharp and blunt edges of a hardy tool.

If a wider piece of steel is being used to forge a deeper blade, a hardy tool can be employed to separate out and forge the tang. This method is chosen when making chef's knives, which have a wider blade.

The following precautions should always be taken when using a hardy tool as it is potentially very dangerous:

- Never leave the hardy in the anvil as it has a sharp edge and you could catch yourself against it as you forge.
- Remove the hardy from the hardy hole as soon as you have finished using it.
- Hold the hammer with a longer gap between your hand and the hammer head so that if you miss a blow on the hardy you do not hammer your hand into the sharp edge of the hardy, which could cut a finger off. Always make sure you are holding the end of the handle when using a hardy tool in order to keep your hands away from the sharp edge. This will make the hammer feel heavier in the hand, so if necessary you can use a lighter hammer for this process.
- Try to make single hits, placing the hammer where you want to hit and then lifting and hitting the steel. It is very easy for the steel to jump from its correct position. Fast multiple blows can cause multiple cuts in the steel, which need to be removed when grinding.

When forging a tang using a hardy tool, start by marking out the material with engineer's chalk, in this case at 2cm from the end. The steel is then forged over the sharp blade of the hardy, cutting to a depth of no more than one-third of the way through the steel.

The tang transition area is then flattened on the anvil, hammering in any bulges in the steel. Place the steel over the rounded section of the hardy and force the cut over it to a depth of no more than halfway through the steel. Leave enough material at the base of the tang where it meets the blade and gives a rounded transition between blade and tang.

The steel is held at a low 45-degree angle from vertical and forged straight down on to the corner of the bar. This action opens up the L shape of the tang material. Ideally this needs to be done over a square edge of the anvil.

Any excess thickening that forms in the tang should be forged as soon as soon as it is noticed. Make sure in particular that the corner of the separated tang area does not fold over and become a cold shut.

The rest of the tang is forged as described in the previous section.

Once the tang has been forged, check around the inside corner formed between the tang and blade to ensure there are no rips or nicks that might cause the tang to crack where it meets the blade. Any nicks should be removed from the tang with a small round file or with a grinder. When this has been done the blade is ready for the next stage of forging.

The correct way of holding a hammer to keep the hand safe when using a hardy tool.

Marking the steel with engineer's chalk.

The steel is forged over the sharp edge of the hardy tool to a depth of one-third of its thickness.

Forging over the rounded section of the hardy tool to a depth of half the material thickness.

Forging out the separated tang material.

The blob of tang material is then forged into the tang shape.

Check the tang for folds or nicks.

The finished tang.

FORGING THE PREFORM SHAPE

Before forging the blade bevels it is advisable to forge a preform blank. This is a simple outline of the blade shape we are making. We know that the blade will gain more width when we forge the bevels into it, so the preform needs to be more pointy than the finished knife is. The preform ought to be relatively even in thickness, since this is intended to be forged into a knife blank that does not yet need to be bevelled or too thin.

When forging the blade tip, stand right next to and slightly around the anvil, working the end of the bar on the far side of the anvil. The hammer is then able to cross the airspace past the edge of the anvil and so forge a point without hitting against the face of the anvil. Brace the tongs against your hip to resist the force of the hammer blows hitting backwards into the steel.

Holding the tang with tongs, the blade tip is forged back into the blade from the end of the bar. It is important that this is done from the end of the bar and not just simply hitting the top of the bar downwards. If the top of the bar is forged down, the end will be forced into a 'fish mouth' shape and the resulting fold-over will have to be removed by grinding.

You will find that there is a sweet spot that makes this forging much more efficient. If the end of the bar is hit at slightly less than 45 degrees, the force from the hammer blows holds the steel against the anvil. At any higher angle the material will be knocked back into your tong hand.

As you forge it the tip will become thicker and this must be forged out as you work. Be very careful not to forge the tip any thinner than the blade stock's original thickness.

Having a little extra thickness in the material allows potential for the blade to be shaped when it comes to adding the bevelling. If you forge too thin at this stage it will not be easy to alter the shape of the knife you are making.

Gradually extend the taper back along the blade. It is much easier to make a stubby blade shape and then gently extend it.

Work the stubby point into a longer bevel, remembering to forge the intended thickness back into the blade. The finished preform should be both elegant and 'pointy'.

Once you are happy with the preform shape you are ready to forge the knife blade bevels.

The preform blade shape should be even in thickness.

When standing at the anvil to forge the tip, make sure the body is forward and that you are hammering back towards yourself.

Hitting the bar from the top down will force the end out into a 'fish mouth'.

Striking the end at the sweet spot angle of less than 45 degrees will help avoid fish mouth distortion.

The stages of forging the blade profile.

FORGING THE BLADE BEVELS

The purpose of blade bevelling is to forge the rectangular-sectioned blade preform into a truncated triangular blade section with a single bevel running from the spine to the edge of the blade. This needs to be the same on both sides of the blade. It is also usual practice to create a distal taper on the blade. This is a taper that runs from the thick blade where it meets the tang to the thinner tip, which makes for an elegant blade weight distribution in the finished knife.

The aim is also to secure a good blade profile with enough thickness in the blade that it can later be ground thinner. I forge my edges down to around 2mm thick, knowing that at least 0.5mm will be ground from each side of the blade in the course of pre-heat-treatment grinding, which will give an edge thickness of at least 1mm when the blade is hardened.

To ensure the blade bevel is at the correct angle, the spine of the blade is lifted by 1.5mm and hammered at an angle.

Hold the blade preform near the edge of the anvil, with the edge of the blade toward your hammer hand. Lift the back edge of the blade fractionally by between 1 and 2mm and angle your hammer blows to create a wedge-shaped starter bevel at the edge of the blade. The purpose of creating this small bevel is to see if the angle at which the blade is held on the anvil is correct and that the bevel being forged on top of the blade by the hammer is equal to the bevel being forged by the anvil on the underside of the blade. It is a subtle process, although the blows should be hard enough for the results of the individual impacts to be visible in order for you to decide if the angles are correct.

Hold the steel near the edge of the anvil so that the hammer blows can overlap the edge of the anvil rather than smashing into the anvil face. Make sure that you are lifting the opposite edge of the steel. Forge the bevel with angled blows, ensuring that the hammer hits the same place on the anvil blow after blow.

A correct distal taper.

Move the steel under the hammer rather than moving the hammer along the blade, trying to hit the same place on the anvil each time. What you are trying to do is to forge as evenly and repetitively as you can, as though like a human power hammer, with blow after blow coming down at exactly the same angle.

Forge a few centimetres of the blade like this and then have a look at the bevel on both side of the blade. The top bevel is formed by your hammer blows on the blade, the bottom bevel is formed by the action of the anvil on the blade. It is worth keeping this in mind whenever you forge. It is easy to think that it's just the hammer forging the steel, but it is in fact the hammer and the equal and opposite action of the anvil that together forge the steel.

Keep checking to ensure that the bevels are extending the same distance up both sides of the blade. If they are the same and the forging seems central to the edge as you look down it, carry on extending the bevel around the edge of the blade,

A correctly proportioned blade bevel with an edge about 1mm thick.

Positioning the blade near the edge of the anvil when blade bevelling allows the hammer to be in free space by the anvil instead of hitting it.

The position of the blade on the anvil for bevelling seen from above.

The top bevel is forged by the action of the hammer.

The bottom bevel is forged by contact with the anvil.

using the starter bevel as a reference. Hold it flat on the anvil so that you can continue at the same angle along the blade.

If the bevels are not the same on both sides of the blade, however, you need to think about what it is that you are doing wrong. If the bevel on the top of the blade (where the hammer is forging) is longer than the bevel on the bottom (where the anvil is forming the bevel), it is likely that you are holding the blade at too high an angle and you need to lower the spine of the blade closer to the anvil.

An extreme version of where the angles are way out of true can be seen where the top of the blade has no angle and there is a very small angle on the bottom. To avoid this it is necessary to lower the blade angle.

If the bevel on the top of the blade (where the hammer is forging) is shorter than the bevel on the bottom (where the anvil is forming the bevel), it is likely that you are holding the blade at too low an angle and you need to raise its angle.

The angles formed by bevelling are very important for a number of reasons, so it is worth paying attention to them all the way through the forging process. The closer you get to having the angles perfect, the less trouble will be generated by warping during the grinding and heat treatment of the blade.

As the blade bevel is forged, the blade profile starts to bend away from the edge of the knife. Forging the edge makes it thinner and the blade wider. The edge also becomes longer than the spine, so the blade will need to be straightened. This task must be repeated again and again.

In its simplest form straightening a bend in a blade is carried out by imagining the bend as a bridge. Both ends of the bend are supported and the middle of the bridge is hammered down. When straightening a bend formed by bevel forging, take care to share the hammer blows along the whole edge of the blade so as not to dent the thin edge too heavily.

End-on view of a plasticine model blade showing even bevels.

Lowering or raising the blade to change where the bevels form on the blank.

If the blade was held too high, the top bevel formed by the hammer will be larger than the bottom bevel formed by the anvil.

If the blade was held too low, the top bevel formed by the hammer will be smaller than the bottom bevel formed by the anvil.

During bevel forging the edge is stretched, causing the blade to bend.

Straightening the bend in the initial stages of bevel forging.

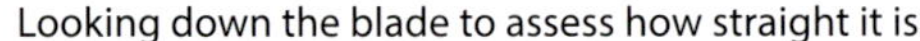

Looking down the blade to assess how straight it is.

Untwisting the blade in a vice.

Straightening the blade by forging on the flat.

When the blade's profile has been straightened, you should also check the straightness of the rest of the blade. I tend to look at the spine and the edge individually when looking for wobbles or bends. Sight down the blade as if you were aiming a gun and look for any bends. It helps to hold the blade against a light background as any warps and bends will show up more clearly this way.

Start by straightening the spine of the blade, as it is thicker, and then go on to straighten the edge.

I would always straighten the blade hot, since when finishing off the blade you can reduce the heat to a dull red as you get closer to a straight blade. The real trick of straightening is to hit the blade once and then look to see if that is enough. If not, hit it once again. More than one hit is likely to leave you with a blade that has bent the other way.

If the blade is twisted you can put the hot blade in a vice and untwist it with a pair of tongs. Untwisting will often leave the blade a little bent, so some straightening will be needed after the twisting.

Straightening is probably the most complex aspect of forging a blade and it must be addressed again and again.

Once the blade has been straightened, proceed with further forging of the bevel and then re-straightening. Repeat these steps until the blade edge starts to get too thin to be safely hammered on the edge. This is normally when it reaches about 2.5mm edge thickness. After this point I change my process and consider other ways of forging of the blade that will allow the edge to become a little thinner and enable the blade bevel to be forged all the way up the blade width to the spine.

Forging the bevel near the edge makes the blade thinner and stretches it out width-wise, but it also gets longer and the blade bends away from the edge. Start by forging the centre of the blade with the hammer held at the same bevel angle as was used on the edge. Forging the middle of the blade will not change the outline shape of the blade that much, but it will make the blade thinner in the middle, wider and longer. Keeping the same angle, change the hammer blows to striking the spine. This will make the spine material thinner, while also making it spread wider and longer, helping to straighten the blade.

If it is necessary to bend the blade profile shape towards the edge, forge along the spine and middle to the left of centre. If it has to be bent away from the edge, forge the edge and middle to the right of centre.

The result of this forging should be a straight blade. You will also end up with the blade bevel extended all the way from the edge to the spine of the blade, giving a distal taper down the length of the blade.

Straightening the blade towards the edge by forging the spine and middle.

Straightening the blade towards the spine by forging the edge and middle.

Once I am finally happy with the blade thickness and blade bevels I tend to turn the blade around and hold the blade tip in my tongs. I then finish forging the beginning of the blade and the tang.

When I make knives I generally forge the blade section profile (a truncated triangular section) all the way through the tang so that the tang has the same profile section as the blade.

The final stage of forging the blade is to straighten it. Start with the profile, making sure the tang is true to the centre line of the blade. Then look for any warps or wobbles in the tang and straighten those. Straighten the spine and finally the edge. Remember that there will be two tapers on the blade, one from the beginning of the blade to the tip and one from the beginning of the blade along the tang (the whole blade has a slightly diamond-shaped section when looked at from the spine along the tang). Both tapers must be straightened separately and then made true to one another.

Once you have confirmed that the blade is straight, it is ready to grind. My usual practice, however, is to perform a normalising cycle on the blade first, so it would be a good idea to look at heat treating before going on to the grinding of the blade.

The finished forged blade.

loosen

CHAPTER 4

GRINDING THE BLADE BEFORE HEAT TREATMENT

Before we start grinding it is worth reaffirming what we are hoping to achieve when grinding the blade. The process of grinding is split into two distinct stages: before and after heat treatment.

The aim during the first stage of grinding is to produce a cleaned-up version of the forged blank, with the bevel grinds following the bevels that have been set up during forging. The goal is to grind an even edge thickness and an even distal spine taper, while trying to keep as much of the thickness as possible.

At this stage we are not trying to grind a finished thin-edged knife. The thickness allows any warping that might occur in the heat treatment to be corrected. The thicker the blade is the less likely it is to warp during heat treatment, leaving more material available to allow for grinding the blade straight. The minimum edge thickness before heat treating ought to be 1mm.

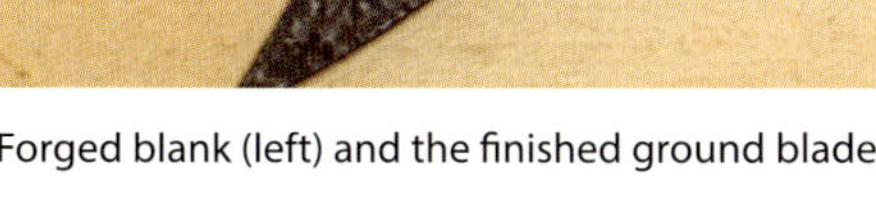

Forged blank (left) and the finished ground blade.

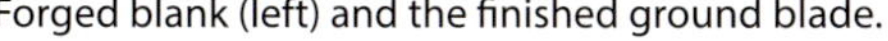

The author at work at a belt grinder.

After the blade has been fully heat treated it is possible to get the blade to its finished dimensions with a thin edge below 0.5mm (and sometimes thinner). Once the blade has been ground to dimension it is ground again to remove the coarse grinding scratches. This is followed by hand sanding and sharpening the finished blade.

The most important thing to consider when you start grinding your bevels is that the belt grinder will remove skin and flesh as easily as it will remove metal. I always maintain a safety space of around 2.5cm between my fingers and the edge of the belt and *I never grind with my hands in front of the belt.* Please keep to these rules to keep your hands safe. I run a no-gloves rule on my grinders as the risk of having a glove pulled into the machine belt has much more dire consequences that just losing some skin. Belt grinders are dangerous tools and you must always concentrate on what you are doing when you use one.

I do all my pre-heat treatment grinding at 24 or 36 grit (the coarsest grits available). It takes a powerful grinder to make the most of 24 grit, so I would recommend starting with 36 grit. Use the coarsest grit you can to remove as much material as possible. Coarser grit also generates less heat. Discard belts as soon as they are no longer cutting well. I find that fast work is much more important than getting the most from a belt.

Before starting grinding it is worth offering up the blade bevels against the grinder platen with the grinder turned off to see how it feels. Hold the blade edge up, at least to start with. The edge is the thinnest part of the blade and this will give an indication of its thickness. Hold the bevel flat against the grinder and feel the bevel or bevels on the blade. Take the blade away from the belt and then return it, feeling its place on the platen once more. This will give you a good feel for the angle of the bevel on the grinder.

Stand close to the grinder with your elbows braced against the side of your body. This will enable you to have a controlled hold on the blade. If you hold your arms out in front of you, you will have far less control over the grinding.

Ensure your fingers are a safe distance from the belt.

Before you start grinding feel the position of the forged bevel on the grinder.

Correct and incorrect positions at the grinder. Holding your arms out to act as long levers makes the grinding harder.

Where you place your thumbs when grinding will dictate which part of the blade will be ground. In its simplest form this will be the part of the blade placed between your thumbs. Remember that if the blade has a high tang or tip you will have to take measures to even out the pressure of your thumbs by placing one thumb or the other towards the edge.

When grinding a blade heat is generated by friction with the belt. It is very important that the blade is regularly quenched in water. When you are grinding the blade in its pre-heat-treated stage there is no risk of the blade overheating, but you will burn yourself if you do not regularly quench the blade.

The first intention when grinding is to establish an area of good form on the blade with one single bevel from the spine to the edge of the blade. When grinding you should frequently check the blade edge thickness, the spine thickness and the evenness of the single bevel. Reference these three features every few seconds or the blade can easily be ground too thin.

Start by grinding the area of the blade where the bevel has been most evenly forged. If the bevel does not run from edge to spine – there is often a small extra bevel on the underside of my forged blades – change the placement of your thumbs to alter the grind.

The way you change the area being worked is subtle but also quite simple. If you want the grind to move towards the spine, move your thumbs very slightly down the blade towards the spine. If you want the grind to move towards the edge, move your thumbs very slightly up the blade towards the edge.

Once a single bevel has been established on one part of the blade, start moving it along the blade, using the first area of good form as a 'feel reference' and superimposing that single bevel on the rest of the blade.

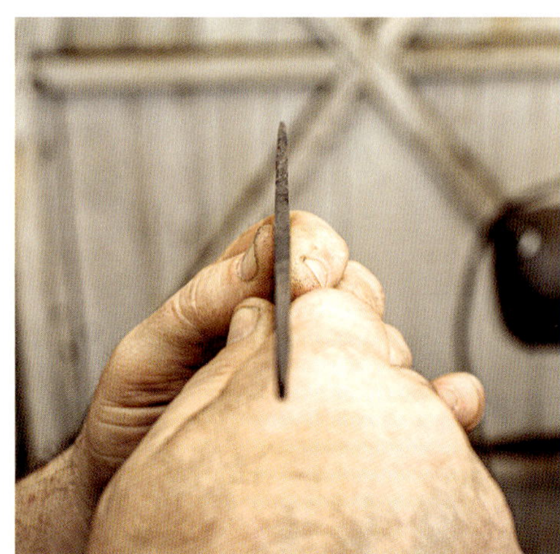

When grinding the blade you should frequently check the state of (left to right) the bevel, the edge and the spine.

In this manner work along the blade, feeling the full bevel as it contacts the grinder platen. Move along the length of the blade, making sure that each new area has good form that can be used as a feel reference before moving on to the next.

It is my practice to grind in one direction at a time, never back and forth along the blade. This takes me from the area of established good form towards the tip. As a separate stage I then move from the area of good form towards the tang. Try to avoid grinding backwards and forwards, as it is very easy to let inequalities from both ends of the blade influence your grind. This will often result in multiple bevels on the blade or sometimes a subtle convex grind.

On most of the blades I make there is no difference between the grinding angle used for the blade and that for the tang. When I grind the beginning of the blade I just carry on through the tang without changing the grinding angle.

When you reach the tip of the blade or the tang, however, it is necessary to change the approach to prevent your thumbs being fed into the grinder.

Tip grinding can seem complicated and certainly needs practise. Make sure that the area just before the tip is well ground with an established single bevel. Change your hand position, holding the middle of the blade and tang (or tip), and then stand to one side of the grinder. Present the already ground area

Making the initial grind.

Moving your thumbs towards the edge moves the grind in that direction.

Moving your thumbs towards the spine moves the grind that way.

to the platen, contacting the area of good form and using it as a reference before moving the grind to the tip of the blade.

If anything goes wrong when grinding, return to a part of the blade with good form and try again moving the good form along the blade until the area next to the tip is good.

Because blade grinding on a belt grinder is a blind operation (that is, you cannot see the other side of the blade against the grinder's platen), it is really important that you check the results frequently, examining the edge thickness, spine thickness and state of the single bevel. The whole process is a feedback loop. You must look at what you have done and then decide whether the grind is right or wrong. If it's good carry on, but if it's not you should remedy the situation, normally by going back to an area of good form on the blade and using that as a reference for the grind.

If you end up grinding multiple bevels onto a blade, it will show a number of facets and it will become quite difficult to tell which part of the blade you are currently grinding.

Grinding from side to side is not recommended.

Good practice: (left) grinding from an area of good form towards the tang; (right) grinding from good form to the tip.

There is usually no need to change the grinding angle on the blade and the tang.

Position of the hands for tip grinding.

If there are multiple bevels it can be hard to see where you are.

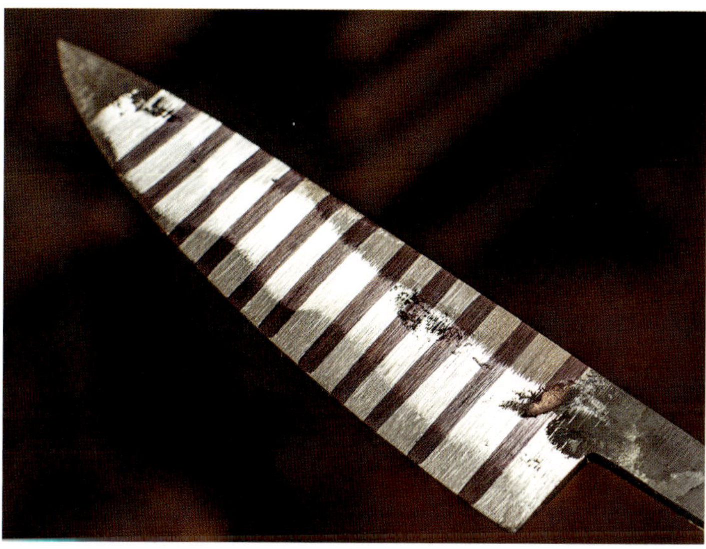
Marking the blade with permanent marker to help identify the areas that have been ground.

Grinding out multiple bevels by removing ink at the centre of the blade.

Feeling the multiple bevels on the grinder,

Push stick

There are a couple of tips that can help correcting the problem of multiple bevels. Once you have ground a single bevel everything becomes much easier as you can use that bevel as a reference for the rest of the grinding.

Marking the blade with permanent marker, for example, will show you exactly where you are grinding so you have a better idea of how to alter the bevels you are making.

In order to fix multiple bevels, grind the centre bevel of the blade until it grows larger and larger and eventually becomes one bevel from spine to edge. If you lose any sense of exactly where you are grinding, mark it with pen repeatedly. This can be particularly useful when grinding the blade tip, as you can mark it with pen, see exactly where you are grinding and then creep your grind up towards the tip.

Another way of tackling multiple bevels is to hold the blade against the grinder platen with the grinder turned off. You can then rotate the blade until you feel all of the bevels against the platen. As you do this, make a note of how far the edge is from the belt, or more specifically the size of the shadow the blade casts upon the belt. This will provide both a feel reference and

Correct position of holding the blade against the belt with a push stick while holding the tang in the other hand.

Cleaning up the intersection of the tang and blade using a push stick.

a visual reference, which can help you find the mid-point bevel on the blade that will allow you to grind back to a single bevel.

If I were grinding the blade I would probably profile the blade before grinding the bevels into it, because I am confident that I would not over-grind the edges. If you are still learning, however, grinding the bevels first allows you to grind back into the blade edge when you profile the blade. That method will create some more thickness that will enable you to re-grind the bevels.

Whichever way is used, I would always grind the profile of my blades before heat treatment.

When profile grinding, hold the blade tang in one hand with the blade at an angle to the belt, so that your hand is not in front of the grinding belt. In the other hand you can then hold a push stick, which is placed in front of the grinding belt.

A push stick is a piece of wood used to distance and protect your hand from the grinding belt. I usually cut a couple of crossed slits in one end and put a step in the other. The slits help to prevent the blade from rotating in your hand when profile grinding. One slit is cut to fit the edge width and the other to fit the spine thickness. The notch can be used to support the spine or edge of the blade when grinding bevels or cleaning up the tang bevel.

Hold the blade on the grinder at an angle. This prevents the hand holding the tang from being ground by the belt. It also stops you wearing away a strip on the grinding belt.

When grinding the blade profile it is really important that you grind with the blade point trailing against the direction of the belt travel. If you point the blade tip in the direction in which the belt is travelling, it may pierce the belt and could be dragged from your hand with disastrous consequences.

Cleaning up the blade profile will give a good idea of the edge thickness of the blade. When the blade has an even edge thickness, ideally no less than 1.5mm thick, and an even distal taper to the spine, it is then ready to be heat treated.

The blade does not have to be perfectly ground and flaw-free at this stage as more material will be ground from the blade after heat treatment. It is important that you cannot feel any marks or dents left from the forging when running a finger along the flat of the blade. Any that can be felt will need to be ground out before heat treatment. Any deep marks, in particular, will make the cooling during heat treatment very uneven.

If you are happy with the evenness of the blade outline and thickness, it is then time for the next stage, heat treating.

Grinding the blade profile using a notched push stick.

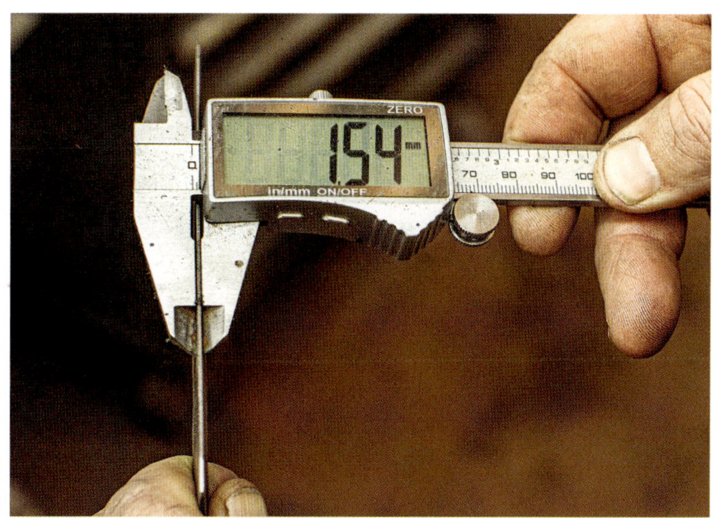

An even blade ready for heat treatment.

CHAPTER 5

HEAT TREATMENT

Heat treatment is in many ways the most important part of the process of knife making as it dictates some of the basic physical features of the finished knife, such as its hardness, which has an effect on how it will hold its edge, its toughness, which affects the strength of the blade, and its failure mode (how it might snap or bend). The way the blade has been heated will also have an impact on the grain size of the steel, which will influence the likelihood of the blade cracking.

There are three major stages within the heat treating I use:

Normalising and thermocycling. This process puts the elements from which the steel is formed into a state of solution, reduces grain size in the steel and prepares the blade for hardening.

Hardening or quenching. This causes the steel to become as hard as it possibly can by quenching.

Tempering. This process reduces some of the hardness gained during the quench and adds toughness to the knife.

Heat treating can involve a simple process of following known steps or attempting to understand a vast and complex metallurgical subject.

I will look at the processes I use, both when heat treating in a simple forge and when using more controlled heat-treating furnaces. Heat treating can be done well with basic tools such as a gas forge and kitchen oven, but the chance of successfully repeating your results will increase when more precise temperatures can be controlled with the use of an electronic heat-treating oven.

A glowing blade being quenched.

Whenever faced with a new variety of steel it is always worthwhile to make some test blades and then process them with recommended heat treatments. The adage 'test what you do and then do what you have tested' is never more true than with heat-treating.

My process when heat treating plain carbon 1080-type steel in a forge is to thermocycle the steel three times by heating the steel to a nominal temperature of 800°C and allow it to cool in air. The steel is then hardened by heating it again to a nominal temperature of 800°C and quenching it into oil. It is then tempered between 180 and 250°C in an old kitchen oven.

If the blade has been ground I paint it with an anti-scale compound. This is a clay paint that helps to prevent excessive scaling of the ground blade when it is put back into the forge for heat treating. Anti-scale compound such as ATP-641 can be purchased from knife-making suppliers.

ATP-641 anti-scale compound.

NORMALISING

When forging steel at temperatures higher than about 830°C we are unwittingly growing the grain size of the steel. Since the steel needs to be soft under the hammer, however, it must be heated to temperatures much hotter than this (1,200–1,350°C). The large grain formed at high temperature is detrimental to the strength of the steel and allows cracks to develop more easily through the material. It is therefore important to reduce the grain in the steel. This is done through a process called normalising or thermocycling.

When you are normalising and hardening in a gas forge there are a few tips to observe in order to do the job well. When I was first taught heat treating as a blacksmith I was told to look for a colour in the steel: cherry red. The colour of steel, however, is very hard to translate from one person's experience to another's. I see an orange colour when the steel is at the correct temperature for normalising and hardening. Even though I still come across references to 'cherry red' in books, for me this term is a bit of a nonsense.

There are instead a couple of more accurate methods that can be used to test whether steel has reached the temperatures required for normalising and hardening.

What we are aiming to do with the normalising process is to heat the steel to just above 800°C and allow it to air cool. This allows some of the alloying elements in the steel, which have come out of solution in the steel and formed large alloy carbides, to be dissolved back into solution in the steel and more evenly distributed throughout the steel. We are also reducing the grain size during this process, since large grain is detrimental to the strength and toughness of the steel.

My practice is to normalise a blade three times. The first time I do it at slightly higher than 800°C (at about 830°C large carbides that can leave the blade brittle will be dissolved). This is followed by another two thermocycles as close to 800°C as possible. The really important part of the normalising/thermocycling and heating for hardening is that the steel must not be heated beyond these temperatures. If it is, large grain will grow again and the steel will be more likely to crack.

Comparison of large (above) and small grain in steel.

'Cherry red'.

Testing with a magnet.

Chasing the shadows out of the steel.

Allow the blade to cool on a brick.

Almost all of the tools I have broken in the three decades I have been working steel have shown large grain. Normalising and thermocycling is a step often overlooked when making cheap industrial tools. It is important not to follow their example.

When normalising and hardening in a forge, two methods can be used to judge whether the correct temperature has been reached. Both methods work very well for plain carbon steels. One is testing the steel with a magnet, the other is a visual phenomenon known as chasing the shadows out of the steel.

Heat the forge by turning it up and allowing the interior to reach an even temperature. It is then turned down until it is a dull orange. Since the forge does not generally reach an even heat throughout its interior, the area beneath the burner is often hotter than the surrounding areas. We are looking to heat treat the knives in an environment that is a little hotter than the 800°C required. It is much easier to heat treat when the forge is in the shade, as bright sunlight will make it hard to see some of the subtle things that are happening in the steel.

When steel heats up to a temperature of 770°C it is no longer attracted to a magnet. This is called the Curie point of the steel, the temperature at which the electrons within the steel change the way they spin. Above this temperature the steel is not be attracted to the magnet, but as it cools down below 770°C it becomes attracted once more. This gives a fixed point reference that can be used for judging if the steel is above or below 770°C. Mount a magnet on the side of the forge or anvil so that the weight of the knife blade and the tongs holding it do not interfere with your ability to feel the magnetic attraction of the steel. Make sure the blade is only just touching the magnet and that the latter is not being confused by the attraction of the tongs or indeed the parts of the blade that are still below 770°C.

Getting accustomed to the colour of the steel at the lowest temperature when it stops sticking to the magnet will give a better idea of the kind of orange temperature colour you are looking for.

It is worth noting that the steel can feel semi-magnetic as it gets close to the temperature. By my judgement this characteristic is reached just below 770°C.

Another phenomenon used to judge the temperature of the steel for normalising and hardening is known by old-time blacksmiths as 'chasing the shadows out of the steel'. I like this analogy for a couple of reasons. It has an romantic feel and sounds like something from *The Lord of the Rings*. I also like it because it is describes a real metallurgical phenomenon. Much traditional blacksmith knowledge is wrong from a modern scientific point of view or is anecdotally correct, but not for the reasons that have long been assumed.

In modern metallurgy 'chasing the shadows out of the steel' is called decalescence, a lag in the brightening of the steel that can be observed as it heats up past about 800°C.

What's actually happening in the steel is quite complex. Steel is a solid state solution of carbon in a matrix of iron. Steel also has a crystalline structure. At room temperature it exists in its normal form (pearlite) as a body centre cubic arrangement of carbon in a lattice of iron. As the temperature increases past around the transformation temperature (800°C) the steel changes its structure to a face centre cubic arrangement and can hold more carbon in its matrix. This change is endothermic and requires energy. It is this energy consumption that causes the lag in the steel brightening. As the steel is heated initially it brightens from red to dull orange. It then lags as it passes through decalescence and as soon as the transformation happens the steel then carries on brightening. What we are looking for is a delineated brightening in the steel after a lag in its brightening.

This will normally happen where the steel is thinner as it heats more quickly. My usual way, however, is to try to normalise a blade by heating the largest thermal mass of the blade, then the tip and then the beginning of the blade, before finally turning the blade around and heating the tang. On a smaller blade or a large evenly heated forge the whole blade can get to the correct temperature evenly, but normally it is a case of heating one part of the blade just above the transformation temperature and then another overlapping part.

If you are careful it is possible to get quite close to the optimal temperature while looking for the shadows being chased out of the steel and cross-referencing this with the fixed point reference of the magnet. Of the two methods the magnet is more certain and chasing the shadows out of the steel requires more experience, but if you can master it you are observing the actual phase change taking place in the steel.

When you have completed the three normalising cycles it is time to move on to hardening or quenching the blade.

HARDENING

Hardening the blade is carried out to make the steel as hard as possible. This is done by cooling the steel quickly from above its transformation temperature. This tricks the blade into forming a structure called martensite, which is the hardest structure of steel.

When the steel is heated above its transformation temperature its crystalline structure changes. This high temperature structure is called austenite. When the steel is slowly allowed to cool down to room temperature by sitting in air, the austenite slowly turns into pearlite. This is the soft room temperature state of steel. Pearlite can be bent and if you hit it with a hammer you could dent it. It can be filed and cut with a cold chisel or hacksaw. This happens when we normalise the steel.

When we cool the high temperature austenite quickly by quenching a different structure is formed called martensite. This martensite is a stressed needle-like structure that is very hard but also brittle. If you try to bend fully hardened martensitic steel it will fail by snapping. A file would skate across its surface and it would dull a hacksaw. Hitting it with a hammer would be dangerous as it could shatter. Fully hard martensitic steel is too hard and brittle to be of much use, so it is normally tempered (the third of the heat treatment processes). This tempering reduces the hardness and brings some toughness into the steel.

When going about hardening a blade, check out the two indicators that helped when normalising the blade. Check that the shadows are chased out of the blade and also double check that the blade has become non-magnetic. The blade is then quenched in oil to cool it quickly.

I use a number of different quenching media to quench my blades. For most plain carbon steels I use either canola (rapeseed) oil or a fast commercial quenching oil (*see* Chapter 1). Don't use just any old oil, motor oil (used or new), other industrial oils or olive oil. These are all too slow to use as a quench medium when working with plain carbon steels.

Quenching the blade in oil.

Keep a fire extinguisher, a fire blanket and a piece of steel ready in case the oil catches fire.

The range of oils and other quench media available is numerous and it may be useful to have a choice around if you are working with different blade steels. It is worth remembering that some steels need to be hardened into a very fast quench medium, such as water or brine, and if you are using large stock this may well be the case. I use brine when hardening hammers because, although the chosen steel can be hardened into oil in blade sections when it's a 3 or 4lb hammer, it is not cooled quickly enough to harden, so I quench hammers into brine. There is, however, a much greater risk of the piece cracking when you quench into water or brine. Wherever possible I quench blades in oil.

If you are quenching into oil in very cold weather, preheat the oil to 30°C: very cold oil quenches slowly as the oil does not circulate quickly when it is too viscous.

The rule of thumb is that you should have a gallon (4.5 litres) of oil for every pound (600g) of steel you are quenching.

Because oil is flammable, make a quench tank from steel or use a metal tray, pipe or container. Always have a lid or plate of steel available to place on top of the quench tank if it catches fire.

Never try to extinguish an oil fire with water. It can cause a fiery explosion as the water turns to steam and atomises the oil. Always have a fire blanket and a suitable oil-fire extinguisher to hand (in the UK that would be a type F foam fire extinguisher).

Another thing to look out for when quenching is to keep the oil dry. If you let moisture or rain get into the oil it will form a layer of water under the oil. This can turn to steam if the oil temperature rises above 100°C.

When hardening the intention is to get the blade to a uniform temperature just above that where the shadows are chased out of the blade. When this happens quickly check that the whole blade is non-magnetic. If it does not stick to a magnet I would then briefly put the blade back into the forge to allow for the heat lost when checking with a magnet. Then quench the blade tip first or edge first into oil and hold it under the oil until it has cooled to about 50°C.

Be ready for any flames that might shoot up when the blade is quenched. They should go out when the steel at the surface of the oil has cooled down, but if they do not go out, take the blade out of the oil and put a lid on the quench tank.

After the blade has been hardened, I clean it up with kitchen roll and fine wire wool to remove any oil and loose scale. The blade is then tempered.

Cleaning up the blade.

TEMPERING

Tempering is a very important part of the heat-treating process. When the blade has just been hardened and is fully martensitic the blade is in a very brittle state and unsuitable for use. It would snap, or if used as a knife the edge would chip very easily. To reduce this excessive hardness the blade is tempered. Tempering is a lower temperature process (170–550°C) that allows some of the needle-like martensitic structure to slip, which reduces the hardness. As the tempering temperature goes up so does the reduction in hardness; conversely, the toughness of the blade goes up as the tempering temperature rises.

I currently use a tempering oven, but for many years I only had an old kitchen oven. If you are still in this situation, buy a cheap type K thermocouple and reader and use it to test the oven's temperature, as a kitchen oven can easily overshoot the set temperature when it is heating up.

A reasonable compromise must be found between steel's two opposing features – hardness and toughness – when tempering. This means there is no 'perfect' all-purpose temper. The blade will either be harder and more brittle or tougher and less hard (and less able to hold an edge as a result). The tempering temperature needs to be adjusted according to the intended use of the knife.

I temper at the temperatures below for knives and other items I make when using 1080 equivalent carbon steels. It must be noted, however, that tempering and the end hardness of a blade may vary from maker to maker depending on the attributes they value in a knife blade.

I normally temper knives in the oven for an hour. Some people put their trust in temper colour charts as an indicator when tempering, but I have found them to be very unreliable. As knives are the product of time as well as temperature, I much prefer to rely on a temperature-controlled oven.

Knife blades are best tempered in a temperature-controlled oven for an hour.

Comparing the colours produced in tempering with those on colour temper charts is not a reliable method.

Tempering temperatures for different knives		
Kitchen knife	190°C	Light use. Edge retention very important
General-use knife	220°C	Needs to be tougher but still hold a good edge
Axe or sword	250°C	Impact tools. Important that they do not break
Sword	250°C	Needs to be able to flex and not break
Hammer	250°C and above	Impact tool. Must not be brittle
Springs	400–450°C	No need for excessive hardness, but must retain springy ability to return to shape
Sub-critical anneal	550–700°C	All usable hardness removed. Will make steel drillable

STRAIGHTENING

When the blade comes out of temper check that it is straight. If it is warped it should be straightened in a vice while the blade is still hot. When the blade is at tempering temperature it will still be springy, but a little plastic deformation can be introduced if the blade is flexed and held for a few seconds in the opposite direction to the original bend.

Flex the blade, hold this position for a few seconds and then release it. Repeat this action a few times if needed. Each time you should flex it a little further or hold it a little longer. There is only a short window when the blade is hot enough to be straightened. If the blade is still not straight after a few attempts, put it back in the temper oven for fifteen minutes at its tempering temperature and repeat the process.

There is a very real risk of snapping the blade if you overflex it, so make sure that you are wearing safety glasses or a face shield.

Straightening can be a very frustrating part of bladesmithing. It takes quite a lot of practice to get it right and even then blades can break. I've broken more than a hundred blades in my years of making knives. It is just part of the process. Keeping some thickness in the blade before hardening makes it much less likely that a blade will warp.

Straightening the blade in a vice.

At tempering temperature the blade can be flexed for a few seconds in the opposite direction to the original bend.

Checking that the blade is straight.

If you overflex the blade there is always the risk that it will snap. Make sure that you are always wearing safety glasses or a face shield.

HEAT-TREATING OVENS

Most of the blades I make are heat treated in ovens designed for this purpose. While it is possible to get good results from heat treating in a forge, there is much less variability from blade to blade if you use a temperature-controlled heat-treating oven.

The process is very similar to what is done in a forge, except the exact temperature can be set. One of the big advantages of a heat-treating oven is that batches of blades can be done at the same time. This makes a huge difference as it is nearly impossible to heat treat more than one blade at a time in a forge.

When working with 1080-type steel the overall process involves the following stages:

1. Paint anti-scale compound on the ground parts of the blade and allow to dry.
2. Normalise no. 1 at 830°C.
3. Allow to air cool.
4. Normalise no. 2 at 800°C.
5. Allow to air cool.
6. Normalise no. 3 at 800°C.
7. Allow to air cool.
8. Hardening to 800°C for quench.
9. Quench into fast quench oil at 30°C.
10. If you are tempering in the same oven as you used for hardening, you must allow the temperature to drop to the tempering temperature before starting to temper the blade.
11. Temper at the required temperature (190°C for a kitchen knife) for one hour.
12. Straighten the blade, if necessary. Then proceed to post-heat-treatment grinding.

When using a heat-treating oven you can be sure that the blade is at the correct temperature.

CHAPTER 6

GRINDING THE BLADE AFTER HEAT TREATMENT

When the blade has been normalised, hardened and tempered – and then straightened if necessary – it will then be ready for post-heat-treatment grinding.

The main purpose of grinding after the heat treatment is to get the edge of the blade down to a suitable thickness so that it can be sharpened. Keep in mind that the area behind the edge must be thin enough to pass through the material that is being cut. The sharpness of the edge will cut the material, but it is the thickness just behind the edge that dictates how easily the blade will pass through the medium being cut. This will vary, however, according to the intended purpose of each type of blade. There is little point, for example, in making a kitchen knife that is so thick behind the edge that it will split open an apple or crack a carrot in half. As a rule I aim for a final edge thickness of no more than 0.5mm when grinding after heat treatment. The spine should also be sufficiently thick to keep the blade stiff enough for its intended purpose. I am generally aiming for an elegant, slim knife that feels light in the hand.

Obviously there are exceptions to this. To an extent we are trying to balance two contrasting requirements of a knife blade: it needs to be both thin enough to cut and thick enough to be stiff.

This knife profile has a thin edge and thick spine.

Grinding the edge of the blade to a suitable thickness. Note the sparks being generated and the need for protective equipment.

Bear in mind that small increases in the blade thickness will have a large effect on the stiffness of the blade. There is a direct relationship between how thickness affects the stiffness of the blade: increasing the blade's thickness by a factor of two will quadruple its stiffness, so even small changes in the blade geometry can have a big effect.

As well as defining the edge thickness, any bulges or warps need to be ground out of the blade. If the blade is very warped it may need straightening again and can be put back into the oven to temper. I normally heat blades at temper temperature for about twenty minutes before straightening. The blade can then be straightened in a vice by bending against the curve while it is still hot. If the blade is a little bent but straight enough to grind true, then it may be worth considering grinding it straight before addressing the edge thickness.

Check the blade visually for straightness and consider how material can be removed to find the true straight blade within the warp. Grind away any material outside of that true line. This will normally be the apex of the bend on one side and then the beginning and end on the other side. This is one of the fundamental reasons why thickness is left in the blade before heat treatment. It is far safer to grind a blade straight than it is to bend it straight at tempering temperature, since every time you straighten a blade you risk breaking it.

The first stage when grinding after heat treatment is to use a coarse belt. The grinding process at this stage is fundamentally the same as previously (*see* Chapter 4), although you must now pay a lot more attention to the blade overheating. If the blade is now overheated you will ruin the temper.

I am very careful to quench the blade regularly in water as I grind. Pay close attention to the evaporating film of water on the blade. As soon as it evaporates the blade must be quenched again. I am more thorough about quenching a blade that has been heat treated and make sure it is not steaming when lifted out of the water. If it is steaming, it should be left in the water for a few more seconds until it loses its heat.

A bent blade that will need grinding straight.

If a blade being cooled in water is still steaming when taken out, it should be dunked again to cool for a while longer.

When the blade is being ground it will tend to overheat on the edge as this is the thinnest part of the blade. The most vulnerable parts of the blade are the tip and heel, which are unable to transfer their heat to the rest of the blade mass and will overheat easily. When working on these areas you must do so in short bursts, thoroughly dipping the blade between grinds.

When steel heats up because of the friction from grinding, layers of oxide form on the steel. These are generated as the steel heats and change as the steel gets hotter or is heated for longer. Some people use them as an indicator for tempering, but I have found that they are not that accurate. They are a very good indication, however, that the steel has been overheated. The oxide colours start with a yellow straw colour and then pass through brown, purple, peacock blue, an iridescent purple, a dull blue and finally metallic grey. The only colour visible on the blade that is in any way acceptable is the yellow straw colour. When making most types of blades any other colour will indicate a softened blade. Often when the temper colours are encountered on a blade it is not a warning about impending overheating. Unfortunately it is an indication that the blade has overheated and therefore ruined, as it is often too thin to re-harden. Keeping the blade cool is really the most important part of post-heat-treatment grinding.

There is a trick that is especially useful on thin blades like kitchen knives to help keep the blade cool. The trick is to grind upside down with the thin edge of the blade pointing downward. When grinding in this way a small pool of water gathers along the edge of the blade and bathes it for a little longer, keeping the edge cooler for quite a while longer. This can extend the grind time between quenches by quite a bit and also make it a lot less likely that the blade edge will overheat.

By angling the blade towards the tip or the heel of the blade, the drip can be sent towards those areas, so extending the amount of grinding that can be done on these areas, which can easily overheat.

As you get closer to the finished thickness remember that the thinner material will overheat more easily, so the only way to go is slowly and carefully. It is inevitable that you will overheat blades, so do not be too hard on yourself when you start.

If you have a grinder with variable speeds, turn the speed down as the blade becomes thinner.

When holding a blade to the grinder, if all the water has evaporated from the blade it is an indication that the blade is heating up.

The range of oxide temper colours that develop on a blade is a sign that the blade has been overheated.

Grinding with the edge down to create a pool of water at the thin edge of the blade.

Grinding with the blade angled and the edge down to create a pool of water at the blade tip.

Grinding with the blade angled and the edge down to create a pool of water at the blade heel.

When the blade is at its desired edge thickness and is straight and even, it is time to move on to finish grinding.

Things change a bit when it comes to the finish grinding of the blade. Up until this point the aim has been to remove material to thin the blade down in a controlled manner. When we move on to finish grinding the intention is to clean up the surface of the blade, removing the deep coarse grit scratches and replacing them with finer and finer scratches until the blade has an acceptable surface finish.

The finishing process goes from using 24 or 36 grit to 120 grit, then a 240 grit linear polish, then a 400 grit linear polish, leading to a hand finish at 400 grit. This is followed by another hand finish with worn 400 grit and an automotive metal polish such as Autosol.

If you have a belt grinder with speed control, it is worth turning it down when starting the fine grinding stages as the finer grits generate more heat due to the smaller grit having more contact and causing more friction.

Finish grinding is a much gentler process than any of those involving coarse grinding, so a slower speed will accommodate this. You should note that 120 grit, in particular, will still remove material so you have to be careful not to overgrind. It is really important to use good sharp belts when you start the finish grind. Worn belts will prolong the work and heat the blade up much more easily than a fresh new belt.

When it comes to the stage of using 120 grit, change the grinding angle to remove all the previous coarse grit scratch marks that run perpendicular to the blade. Tilt the tip of the blade down when changing grit by enough of an angle so that the newer fine scratch marks are visible against the older coarse marks.

When examining the scratches it helps to have multiple light sources or to take the blade into direct sunlight. The intention here is to remove all of the coarse scratches. Start in the middle of the blade and remove the scratches one area at a time. Try to keep the blade angle even so as to present a unified scratch direction. Any change in the angle at which the blade is held will also change the direction of the scratches, making it very hard to see whether old scratch marks are being cleaned up or these are new ones. As always, be careful when grinding the heel or tip of the blade as these will overheat easily.

After all the coarse grit scratches have been cleaned up with 120 grit, the next task is to burn on the handle as the blade is now pretty much at finished dimension and any further fine finishing will be messed up by fitting the handle hot.

A variable frequency drive allows the grinder speed to be turned down.

Grinding at a slight angle, to see the newer scratches against the old coarse scratches.

120 grit scratches overlaid on a background of coarse 36 grit scratches.

A blade finish ground to 120 grit.

BURNING ON THE HANDLE

To burn a handle onto a tang, drill a guide hole for the tang. The hole needs to be slightly longer than the tang and oriented square to the handle. I often hold the blade and tang over the handle in the preferred orientation and then draw around the tang. Next draw a single line along the side of the handle. A guide hole can then be drilled using this line as a reference

A variation on this is to drill two holes and wiggle the drill bits in the holes until there is a tapered guide hole for the tang. The aim is not to make a hole big enough for the tang to fit in, but one that will act as a path of least resistance when the handle is burnt on, so it needs to be smaller than the tang.

For the next stage you will need leather gloves. Since burning in produces a lot of smoke, some kind of mask or an extraction device such as a fan are a good idea to keep the smoke out of your eyes and lungs.

When burning on the handle, the tang is first heated and then the handle hole is pushed over the hot tang. For this I normally use an oxypropane torch, but a plumber's propane torch will do.

Burning on the handle.

Marking where the tang hole will be.

Marking a reference line for drilling.

Drilling the handle block.

Heating the tang with an oxypropane torch.

The blade is clamped into a vice using leather spacers so as not to damage the blade. The end of the tang is then heated with a torch until a glow is just visible. Take care not to heat any hotter than this.

Heating the tang also has the effect of performing a sub-critical anneal of the tang (a high-temperature temper). This leaves the tang soft, meaning it will not snap when over-stressed but will bend instead.

If the tang is heated any further than dull red, there is a small risk that it may auto-harden as it quickly cools, which could leave it brittle.

When the tang has been heated, push the handle onto the tang. When approaching the tang try to line up the handle so that it follows the path of least resistance created by the drilled hole. The handle material should burn away and allow the handle to slip further up the tang. As soon as there is strong resistance to any further movement, remove the wood and re-heat the tang.

If you feel strong resistance it may be that the tang is too cold or that you have managed to burn the tang out from the path of the drilled holes and it has dead-ended. It is important to make sure that the approach to burning on the handle is as in line with the drill holes as it can be.

As soon as a few centimetres of the handle have been burned on, remove your hands from the block and have a good (but quick) look how the handle aligns with the blade. It is hard to get a proper idea of the alignment when your hands are in the way.

Next look at the burned entrance hole on the handle and check that it is positioned where you want it. You can alter the way the tang is burned on by using a sharp-toothed tool for

The handle is pushed onto the hot tang, following the path of least resistance created by the drilled hole.

Check how straight the burned-on handle block is relative to the blade.

opening up holes known as a broach, or by using the hot tang as a file to direct the way it burns into the handle.

Each time you go through the process of heating and burning on the handle it should progress further up the tang. Once the handle is as far up the tang as is wanted, the final burn-on is performed twice as the handle has a tendency to shrink a tiny amount when it cools down.

When the handle has been burned into position, I normally make sure all of the hardness has been taken from the tang and blade transition and heat this area with the gas torch. This is to ensure that the change in hardness in the tang is not at exactly the same place as the change in cross-section from blade to tang. A little heat is then washed into the blade making sure the edge of the knife does not overheat.

When this is done allow both the blade and the handle to cool down before moving on to the next stage of finish grinding the blade, linear polishing.

Check how straight the burned-on tang hole is relative to the handle block.

Any hardness is removed from the intersection of tang and blade as part of heating the tang.

Linear polishing is a way to avoid hours of sanding by hand.

LINEAR POLISHING

Linear polishing on a soft contact wheel using 240 grit has changed the way I make knives. It is one of the biggest time savers I have discovered, shaving hours off the time needed to sand a blade by hand.

Linear polishing requires a soft contact wheel and a grinder with speed control. I have used 40 shore (soft) rubber wheels, canvas wheels of both the flap and compressed type, and felt wheels.

I have settled on using a felt wheel and run a separate grinder with a huge felt wheel for most of my finishing. Any soft wheel with a diameter of more than 150mm, however, will do.

This method should only be attempted on a machine with speed control, since the action of linear grinding on a wheel, with its resultant small area of contact, is really aggressive even if the sanding belt is a fine grit.

Linear polishing on a blade requires quite a bit of practice as the contact area of a wheel is quite small and it is therefore quite easy to overheat or overgrind the edge or dig into the blade. It is this small contact area, however, that makes this such a great way of finishing blades as you can quickly remove horizontal scratches caused by the 120 grit.

I cannot stress too firmly that you must *make sure you are trailing your blade point* when linear polishing. If you do not grind with the direction of the grinder leading away from your blade tip you will run the real risk of having the blade tip puncture the belt and getting dug into the contact wheel. I normally grind the blade tip very gently as it is very easy to overgrind the tip and turn it from a point to a screw driver, overheating it in the process.

Polishing wheels.

Even a large felt wheel has only a very small contact area where the blade meets the radius of the wheel.

The way you apply pressure when linear polishing is just as important as when grinding on a platen. Make a note of the areas where the horizontal grind marks have been removed and concentrate on those where they remain. As always make sure that the blade is regularly quenched.

I find that I get better belt life if I grind dry, so I will often have a rag ready to wipe the blade dry after each quench before the next linear grind.

When all the horizontal grind marks have been removed from the blade I normally change from 240 grit to 400 grit and perform another linear polish with the grinding marks in the same direction as the previous 240 grit polish. From now the sanding becomes a process of blending the scratch marks in the same direction. With practice it is possible to get a finish that is better than hand finishing.

From this point it is possible to take the blade to as fine a polish as you might wish. If you do a good job little (or no) hand sanding should be needed. To make sure, the machine-polished blade can be taken out into daylight and checked for any scratches that remain from earlier in the process. Look carefully at the heel and tip of the blade especially, as these are difficult to clean up on a machine due to the risk of overgrinding.

If you do not have a wheel on which to linear polish with a belt grinder, there is another procedure that can be used to bring your blade to a finish. After grinding the blade at a slight off-perpendicular angle with 120 grit, angle the blade a little in the opposite direction and clean up the 120 grit scratches with 240 grit. Repeat the process with 400 grit, changing the scratch direction. From 400 grit I would move on to hand sanding.

A start has here been made on linear polishing a blade with 240-grit scratches overlaying those made with 120 grit.

The blade must be trailed in the direction the belt is moving so that it does not dig into the belt.

After finish grinding is completed the blade is ready for hand sanding.

HAND SANDING

The trick to hand sanding is to have to do as little as you can. The bench block I use for hand sanding blades is just a bit of 47 × 22mm wood that has been screwed down to a tabletop so it sticks out past the edge of the bench and a blade can be clamped to it.

Clamp the blade to the block firmly with a plastic clamp and make sure that the edge of the blade is within the outline of the block. Most importantly, ensure that the tip of the blade is not sticking out past the end of the block. Even though the blade is not yet sharp, it is thin and will have burrs along the edge that could easily cut you.

Wrap pieces of abrasive paper around a wooden block. Be careful to hold the block with your fingers above the block so as not to present them to the edge of the knife. Start by working on only one side of the blade. Mark any deeper scratches with permanent pen and then sand in a linear direction.

When starting to sand by hand, jump back one grit size from the last used when sanding the knife on the grinder. If that were 400 grit, for example, start sanding at 320 grit. The aim is to remove all of the horizontal 400 grit marks and superimpose a linear polish on the blade by hand.

You will find that abrasives dull very quickly when you hand sand. Get to know the feel of the abrasive cutting and also listen to the sound it makes. As soon as an area of the abrasive is worn away you must move to another area. It is a false economy to persevere with dull abrasives as it is a waste of time. Clean sharp abrasive will get more work done and leave a better finish. In the cause of economy, however, make sure that all of the abrasive is used, turning the block to each face in turn until they have all been used. Then unwrap the paper, turn it around and use the other end of the sheet.

Once all the machine grinding marks have been removed on one side of the blade, turn the blade over and hand-sand the other side. A really useful tip to prevent the bench block from scratching the underside of the blade is to apply wide

Before hand sanding the blade should be clamped to a blade block.

Sandpaper wrapped around a sanding block. Make sure your fingers are at the sides of the block to prevent them accidentally being offered up to the blade edge.

masking tape to help reduce any scratching caused by abrasive dust falling under the blade. Remove the masking tape after you have finished using each grit and replace it with fresh tape every time the blade is turned over.

After the blade has been sanded in a linear direction, follow the same procedure as would be used if the blade were linear polished on a machine. All the sanding is longitudinal along the blade.

Start hand sanding at one grit lower than the machine finish and then progress up through the higher grits, going from 120 grit to 240, to 320, and then to 400 grit. It is possible to go higher than 400 grit, through 600 and even 800 grit, but I have found I really like the finish I get from using 240-320-400 and then polishing the blade with worn 400-grit paper and a dab of Autosol.

Autosol is a chrome polishing paste that helps to clean up and prevent surfacing oxidation, acting as both a lubricant when hand sanding and as a polish. Autosol should not be used on Damascus blades as it is greasy and can resist the action of etching. It provides an excellent finish, however, on plain carbon steel.

The process of polishing with Autosol is exactly the same as normal hand sanding, except using a worn piece of 400-grit paper smeared with a little Autosol. Work in a linear direction with the same action as when hand polishing. You do not need to use much Autosol. Since it is messy, the blade will need wiping down with a paper towel. The end result is a pleasing satin polish. A used blade can easily be restored with worn or fine abrasive paper and some Autosol.

Permanent marker is used on the blade to indicate any deep scratches before hand sanding.

Sanding the blade.

Protecting the blade with masking tape prevents the underside from being scratched.

Autosol chrome polish

Polishing a blade with worn 400-grit paper and Autosol.

The finished blade after hand sanding.

CHAPTER 7

MAKING THE HANDLE

The handle is in many ways the most important part of a knife. It is the part with which we interact and it is always on view, even if the blade is in a sheath. Yet it is often the most neglected part, as the maker's focus is more often on the blade. This is especially true for new makers. I always try to look at a knife as a whole, not just as a blade with a handle fitted.

Handles can be as complex as you like, but I try to keep mine simple and elegant. It is tempting to aim for a curvy ergonomic handle that fits the hand exactly, but for the most part I prefer to keep the form of the handle simple and elegant. This allows your hand to move up and down the handle and so change the way the knife is held, making for a beautiful and functional tool.

A simple handle form.

The finished knife handle.

SHAPING THE HANDLE

When shaping a handle it should always be remembered that it does not exist on its own. Everything is relative to the whole knife, so when checking its shape always consider the blade and handle together.

I have a set approach to shaping handles. Start by squaring the handle to the blade and then grind the corners to create an octagonal, before rounding off the corners to get the final shape. If this is done methodically it is much easier to see if the handle is even and aligned to the blade. As soon as you start to round off the corners it gets much harder to work out where you should be fixing things if the shape is uneven.

I shape my handles on a belt sander, mostly using the platen, but sometimes fitting contact wheels. It really helps if you are able to flip the sander over sideways in order to see the handle outline easily, but if you do not have this facility the process is the same, but just vertical instead of horizontal.

When grinding wood it is really important that the belts are brand new and sharp. Even the smallest amount of metal grinding will dull the sharp cutting edges of the abrasive belts. There is no problem using the belts on metal after a session grinding wood as they will still grind as good as new. Depending on what wood you grind, it is also worth having a belt eraser. This is a raw latex block that cleans the belt and stops it from loading up with wood dust or resin.

Handle grinding creates a lot of dust. Wood dust can be quite bad for you, so you need to wear a dust mask and it may be a good idea to have some form of extraction system.

Wood dust is also very flammable. If a grinder is being used for both wood and metal grinding, the whole grinding area should be thoroughly cleaned to remove any wood dust before grinding metal. First use a brush, then a vacuum cleaner, and finally blow out any dust that may remain in the wood grinding area. The dust gets everywhere, so I take care to blow down the walls as well any as dust on floors and other surfaces.

Start by comparing the handle and blade together and working out what needs to be ground away to square up the handle. Look down the length of the blade, checking that the blade is in line with the handle along the spine and the back of the handle. Also check that the outline of the knife flows well.

Whenever possible I grind with the blade fitted into the handle, because this way I can be more certain that everything is in alignment. Be very careful not to touch the blade against the grinder as this could ruin it.

The blade and the handle should always be considered relative to one another.

Shaping the handle from a block to the finished profile.

When shaping the handle it is much easier to see what you are doing if the belt sander is horizontal.

A latex belt cleaner will keep the belt in good condition.

You may find it convenient to hold the blade while grinding as it keeps that hand away from the grinding belt. Even a 120-grit belt will cut you, so you must be very careful when grinding the handle.

I rarely draw lines while I grind, but some people find that they can be a real help in showing what has to be done.

Clean up one dimension at a time. Start by examining the blade from above and grind away any unevenness from the sides. In order to taper knife handles, slim down the material at the front of the handle.

Examine the side profile of the blade and handle, in particular checking the alignment of the top of the handle and spine of the blade, or more particularly the line of the tang and blade tip. There ought to be a visual flow between these two lines and that normally means keeping them in line with one another.

Once the top line has been done, grind the bottom of the handle. Note that for this process the blade cannot be kept in the handle as it would get ground against the platen. Depending on the angle of the tang and blade, the blade can be turned

Eyeing the knife and handle from above (left) and from the side.

Holding the blade when grinding the handle.

Pencil lines can be drawn on the handle to help show what needs to be ground away.

Grinding the sides of the handle to help centralise it.

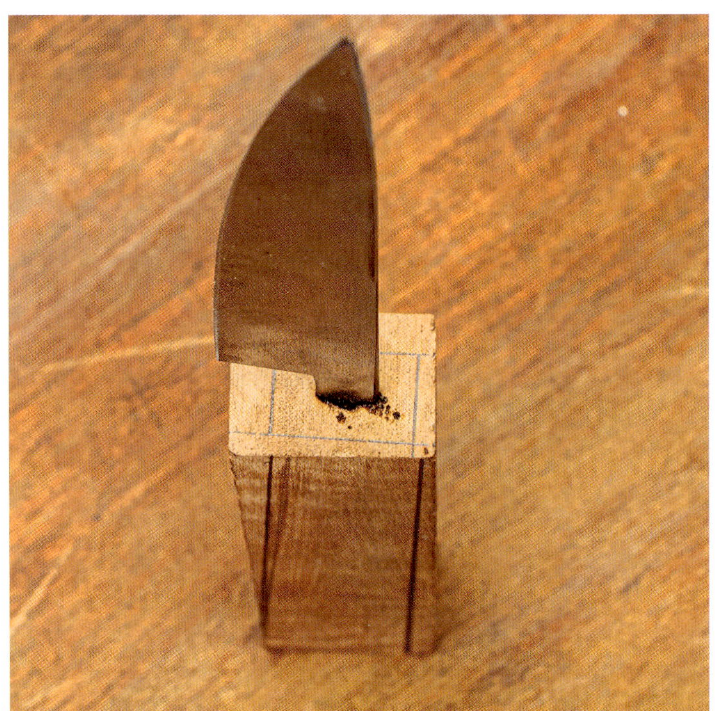

Pencil lines on the handle block are used to establish the grinding positions for a squared handle (left) that can be ground into an octagonal profile.

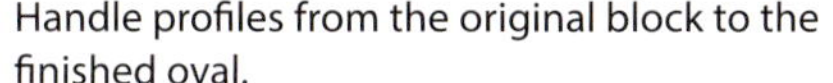

Handle profiles from the original block to the finished oval.

Grinding the barrel shape into the handle.

Removing the 'belly' on the barrel.

around in the handle or a dummy tang is used to hold the blade. Either way you must reference the blade back into the handle to see if the grinding is correct.

While grinding the square handle profile, check that the ends of the handle are square to the blade, Any parallelograms or unevenness found should be corrected at this stage while they are easy to see.

Once you are certain that the handle is all squared up, the next stage is to make the handle octagonal. Most of the knife handles I make are not an even oval but have a slimmer, teardrop-shaped profile where the handle is at its slimmest in alignment with the blade. This allows the slim handle edge to be felt in the hand as a reference for the direction of the blade edge. This handle shape makes for a more user-friendly tool.

At this last stage I normally work the handle block in my hands, trying to shape one end of the handle at a time. Hold the block on the platen at a slight angle so that there is no risk of the end that can't be seen from being ground away accidentally. This should leave the handle with a very subtle barrel shape. The last grind is to remove this barrel when both ends are set. Remember that the handle shape is only relevant when it's on the knife, so check the shape often during this process with the blade in the handle.

The handle is initially shaped using a 120-grit belt. Change the belt over to 240 grit and then take a pass over the handle. It is not the intention to shape the handle at this stage, but to clean up the 120-grit scratch marks.

Once the handle has been shaped and cleaned up on the belt grinder it is time to start hand sanding the wood. Work over the handle with 240 grit with a small bit of paper in your hand, working against the scratch marks left by the machine grinding until they are all gone. Then re-sand using 400-grit paper until a satisfactory finish is achieved. The sandpaper should last a long time and only a small amount will be needed for a handle.

Make sure the sandpaper is new and has not previously been used for metal. Some woods like walnut and oak have a high tannin content and they will become heavily stained when in contact with metal dust. The same goes for your hands. If you have been working steel in the last few days, wear nitrile or latex gloves. In the presence of steel dust walnut turns purple and oak black – so will your hands.

Wood is much more forgiving than steel when it comes to hand sanding and 400-grit sandpaper will leave a great finish on a wooden handle. The extent of the wood grain's beauty will only really become apparent when the handle and blade have been put together and been given a final oiling.

FINAL FIT UP AND GLUING THE HANDLE

Before I glue up a handle, especially when using epoxy, I dry assemble the knife in the handle, checking that the fit is tight and square and that the blade is central to the handle. There should be no gaps where the blade meets the handle. If necessary small wedges made from lollipop sticks cut with a Stanley knife can be superglued in place in the tang hole to hold the blade central and firm. Ideally the blade should not be able to move as it is being glued in place or it will likely set in the wrong position.

Using cutler's resin to fix handles

I use cutler's resin (a traditional hot-melt glue) on many of the knife handles I make. I really like it as a fixing method, but it must be noted that it is not as strong as modern epoxy. As a result there are some applications where epoxy is to be preferred.

I make up my own cutler's resin by heating the ingredients in a pot and cooking them for a while at a low heat before pouring the mixture onto a sheet of greaseproof paper. All of this is usually done outside on a small camping stove as the fumes are potentially flammable. The pot will likely be ruined and from hereon will become nothing but a cutler's resin pot. When it is almost set, score lines into the mixture and break it up into little pieces that are small enough to insert into the handle hole. All of the ingredients listed can be purchased online:

4 parts pine resin
1 part beeswax
1 part carnauba wax
Black iron oxide finely powdered (add as required)

You can experiment with the proportions of the resin to wax mixture as this will affect its toughness, its flexibility and the

The final 'dry' fit up of the handle and blade.

Broken-up pieces of cutler's resin.

melting point of the resin. Remember when the resin is hot it will stick to you and cause a nasty burn.

Handles can be fixed with cutler's resin in the following way. Set up a blowtorch on a bench and put a leather glove on your non-dominant hand. Hold the handle in this hand with the blade inserted loosely. The other hand is free to hold the blade and heat it, feeling for heat on the blade and handle.

Hold the tip of the blade in your non-dominant hand and heat the tang in the torch flame to about just 100–200°C. Try not to actively heat the centimetre of tang closest to the blade as this may cause some temper colours to develop in this area. The intention is to get the heat to creep gently up the blade. Reinsert the blade loosely into the handle and leave it there to allow the hot tang to heat the inside of the handle.

The idea here is to heat the inner faces of the tang hole so that when pieces of cutler's resin are put in the hole they will melt and flow into the wood grain, filling any voids remaining from the drilling and burning on.

The hot blade tang is left in the handle for 30 seconds. The process is repeated until you can feel heat coming through the handle material and the beginning of the blade is too hot to touch. When you are at this stage, fill the handle with cutler's resin pieces and hold it vertical. This is really important as the resin may spill out onto your hand unless the handle is vertical with the hole at the top. Reinsert the hot tang back into the resin-filled tang hole.

Do this gently. If the resin boils, remove the hot tang for about ten seconds and try again, gently pushing the tang into the tang hole. If resin is oozing out of the top of the tang hole when the tang is fully inserted that means there is enough cutler's resin in the handle slot. If you do not see any resin oozing out, remove the tang and place it carefully to the side. Fill the tang hole with more cutler's resin until there is resin pushing up around the tang. Allow the resin to cool down and set. You will notice that the resin pulls into the tang hole a little since it contracts as it cools. Small extra pieces of cutler's resin can be added by gently pushing then against the blade with a lollipop stick while it is still warm.

Do not be tempted to scrape the resin away from the handle blade transition as it is much easier to clean up when it is set hard.

When the resin is set hard, run a thick knife blade along the surface of the front face of the handle. This will cause most of the resin to ping off the handle. Take a clean lollipop stick and

Heating the tang with a blowtorch.

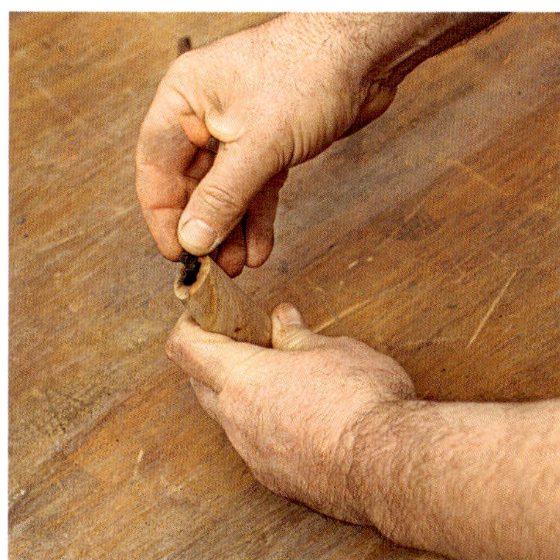
Insert cutler's resin into the hole in the hot handle.

Ensure the handle is vertical when the hot tang is inserted into the cutler's resin that has been placed in the heated handle.

polish the front face of the handle with a fast backwards and forwards motion to generate friction. The cutler's resin will melt and be polished into the front face of the handle. A Dremel fitted with a small polishing mop could also be used for this. The rest of the handle should be cleaned with 400-grit sandpaper.

I really love working with cutler's resin. It is great to use, clean up and finish. It also smells wonderful: I love its earthy aesthetic.

Cutler's resin has the added advantage that if you make a mistake and end up with the blade set in the handle at an angle, you can loosen the blade and handle by putting them in an oven at 90°C.

After the cutler's resin on the front of the handle has been cleaned up, it is time to oil the knife handle. I highly recommend a proprietary gun-stock oil called Birchwood Casey Tru-Oil as the perfect finish for knife handles. Although it takes a few days to do, the results are worth it. There are many other Danish oil-type wood finishes, but this is my favourite.

Try to apply five coats of the oil to the knife handle, allowing about eight hours for each coat to dry. Wear a nitrile glove and apply the oil a couple of drops at a time, spreading it over the handle in a vigorous motion and trying to generate a little heat between your gloved hand and the handle. It is likely the first couple of drops will soak in, so you may need to apply more oil for the first coating. When you are happy that the oil has been worked into the handle, check that there are no drips and there is a smooth layer of oil. Any excess can be wiped off with kitchen roll.

The handle is then placed in a rack, such as one I made from a piece of wood with a series of spaced saw cuts, and allowed to dry for eight hours. This normally means that I am applying oil first thing in the morning and again when I finish in the workshop at the end of the day.

As the coats of oil build up a protective layer of hard cured oil is deposited on the surface. This can have a brilliant shine, which can look amazing.

If you want a high-quality super shine on your handles, I have found that clear boot polish provides an amazing finish. If you want to matt the surface down, however, applying Renaissance Wax and very lightly buffing with 0000 wire wool will give a wonderful matt finish. Any wax applied to the handle is left to dry for a few hours before thoroughly buffing with a clean cloth.

Once the wax polishing is complete the knife is finished apart from the final stropping.

It is easier to remove any cutler's resin around the handle tang area when it has set.

Using a lollipop stick to clean up the handle tang area.

High-grit paper is used to clean up the handle.

Birchwood Casey Tru-Oil provides the perfect finish for handles.

The finished and oiled handle.

CHAPTER 8

SHARPENING THE BLADE

I prefer to sharpen my blade as the last action before I assemble a knife, as it can be very dangerous to interact with a sharpened blade.

Sharpening is an aspect of knife making that is always subject to a compromise between the varied techniques of the sharpening process. The thinner the final sharpened edge angle is, the sharper the knife will be, but if the final sharpened edge is too thin it will flex or chip (depending on its hardness). As the edge angle increases the blade edge becomes stronger, yet the blade is not as sharp and will start to become hard to force through the material that is being cut. That is why a compromise must be found.

The size of the grit used to sharpen the blade affects the smoothness of the cutting edge. A smoother edge means that it is less toothy, which can be an advantage for some kinds of cutting. A cutthroat razor or a woodworking chisel, for example, needs to have a smooth edge to allow for a clean push cut.

There can be an advantage, however, in having some of the toothiness that comes from using a coarser grit, say 240 grit or 400 grit, as the blade will have some kind of saw-like action when draw cutting. This type of edge is particularly good for meat.

The edge I prefer for most of my knives is made by starting to sharpen with a thin edge (0.2–0.5mm) and then sharpening the blade on a slack belt (a belt with the backing platen removed) at 240 grit and then 400 grit. This gives a very slightly convex profile to the edge. An obtuse tough final edge angle on a thin-edged blade gives an edge that is very resilient and still cuts very well. I then finish up by stropping on a polish-loaded leather belt.

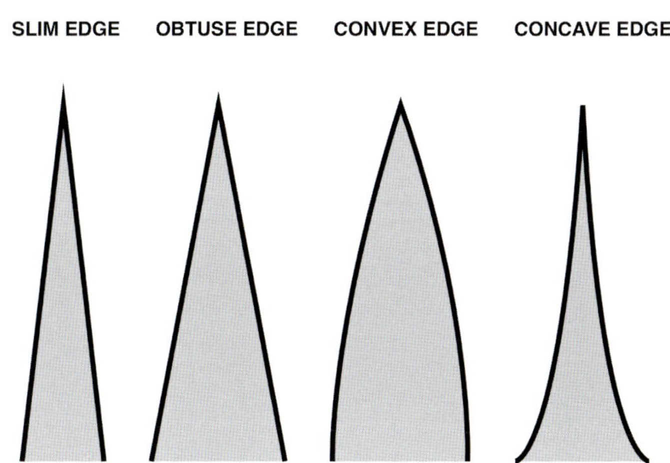

The principal edge geometry variations.

Stropping a knife blade.

Sharpening a knife on a convex belt will give the edge a slightly convex profile.

CONVEX BLENDED EDGE GEOMETRY

My preferred edge geometry is a convex sharpen on a very thin edge (less than 0.5mm)

Convex edge profile.

My initial sharpening is carried out on a belt sander with a 240-grit belt, after removing the grinding platen to reveal a slack belt without a backing. This gives the sharpening profile a very slight convex profile. It is an advantage to have speed control on the grinder when sharpening, as the machine needs to be turned down to a slow speed.

Use a sharp new belt and try to set the belt tension tight. This limits the amount of convex that can be put into the edge grind. The intention is for the edge angle to flow from the edge to the blade and not to be too obtuse.

It is worth remembering that the belts are made of plasticised cloth and that you must not push hard on them when sharpening with a slack belt, as it will change the convex angle of the grinding.

Another thing worth noting is that a slack belt is slightly curved in section (that is, the centre stands proud of the edges). Always try to use this centre of the belt when sharpening.

The first step in sharpening is to polish the edge of the blade. If the edge is blackened from the hardening and tempering, or if it is rusty, it can be very hard to get to the actual edge thickness. Pass the blade horizontally across the belt once or twice until a shiny polished edge is produced.

This edge thickness is then used as a reference to see how close to sharpening the blade might be. If a reflection is visible on the edge of the blade, that means the blade still has some thickness and is not sharp.

One of the tricks that makes a difference to this kind of sharpening is knowing how to hold the blade. Try to present a little ledge for holding the spine of the blade by pinching fingers and thumb together. This ensures that your hand will not be sticking out in front of the blade when sharpening. If your fingers stick out you are very likely to be rather concerned about not grinding them away. That will lead you to hold the blade at an obtuse angle, resulting in a very large final edge angle.

The intention here is to hold the blade at the lowest angle on the belt that does not mark the side of the blade. There should be a gap of no more than 1cm between the blade spine and the belt.

Start by taking a pass along the edge of the blade in both directions. The idea behind this initial sharpening pass is

Sharpening a flowing (left) and obtuse angle.

to remove any burrs that may have been produced by the clean-up passes along the edge. Burrs will result in a confusing impression of how thick the edge actually is. A much more realistic idea of the edge thickness will be had when the burr is gone.

The plan of action I adopt when starting to sharpen a blade is to try to bring any thicker parts of the blade down to the same thickness as any that are thinner, so that the blade's thickness is even along its length. The reference I follow when sharpening is the width of the reflective line along the edge of the blade. As one side of the blade is brought closer to meeting the other, be careful not to over-sharpen the knife. As soon as the reflection from the blade edge is lost in one place that part of the blade is now sharpened. Any further sharpening in that area will only be grinding into the outline of the blade. There is a tendency for this to happen a couple of centimetres into the heel of the blade. This is probably because it is here where one starts putting pressure on the blade. Sharpening is no different to any of the other grinding or forging processes in that you must regularly observe what you are doing and check on your progress pretty much every pass.

When one or more areas are sharp, avoid any further grinding in that area. I normally do this by placing my fingers in that area as I hold the blade. There can be no greater incentive not to grind my fingers and that protects the sharpened blade from being over-sharpened. A less drastic way is to mark the sharpened areas of the blade with a permanent marker to make sure you avoid them. These marks can be removed with thinners.

Bit by bit the whole blade will be brought to a point of being sharp. A full pass should then be made along both sides of the edge on the slack belt. In order to be sure, always take the blade out into direct sunlight in order to check for any signs of a burr along the whole edge of the blade.

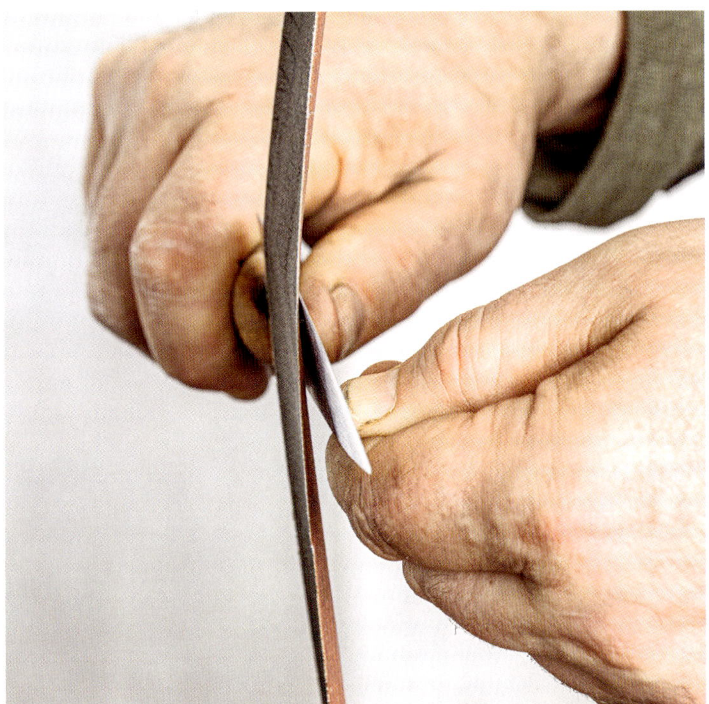

Pushing on the belt changes the interaction angle of the blade.

Passing the blade horizontally across the slack belt.

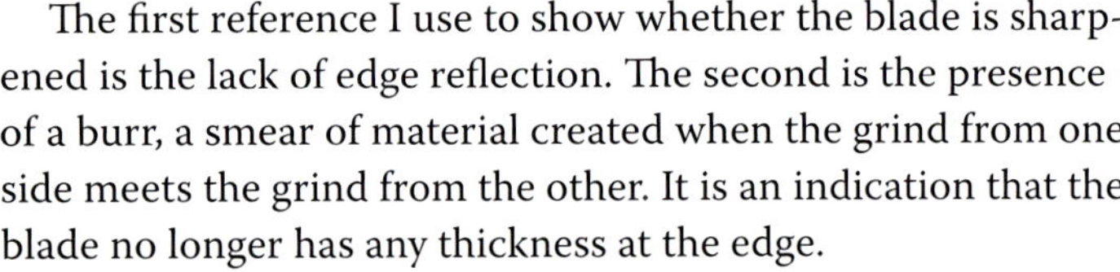

The first reference I use to show whether the blade is sharpened is the lack of edge reflection. The second is the presence of a burr, a smear of material created when the grind from one side meets the grind from the other. It is an indication that the blade no longer has any thickness at the edge.

It should be noted that while these references are very useful when checking the progress of the sharpening, they will not tell you if the angle at which you have ground is optimal. To an extent you can work this out by looking at the distance up the blade your sharpen has ground relative to the initial blade thickness at the edge. When you come to edge stropping you will get a good idea what this angle is since it will be the angle at which the blade bites into the strop.

If the flat of the blade had previously been marked with any grinding marks from when you were sharpening, these should now be cleaned off, but *you must be very careful as the blade is now sharp*. When I clean up a sharpened blade I double-clamp it down within the outline of the bench block. I also wear cut-resistant Kevlar gloves, with another pair of nitrile gloves over the top. Remember that the gloves are cut-resistant, not cut-proof. The nitrile gloves worn over the top are intended to keep the Kevlar gloves clean. Any sharpening slips are cleaned up with 240 grit, followed by 400 grit, and finally a worn 400-grit sandpaper with Autosol polish.

When you have finished sharpening on the slack belt it is time to strop the blade, the final part of the sharpening process.

If a reflection is visible on the edge there is still some way to go.

Pinching your fingers and thumb together when sharpening will keep your fingers behind the blade.

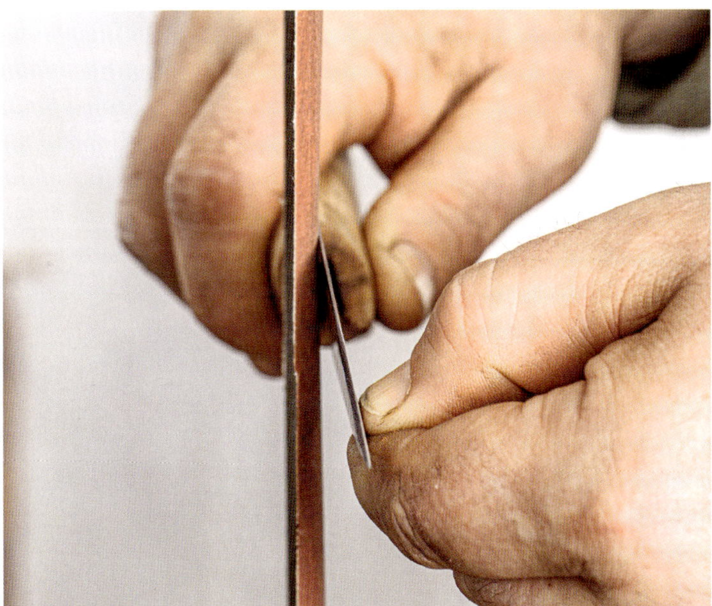

Holding the knife at a low angle on the belt.

Some of the areas on this edge are sharp and others are near that state.

Any burrs on the blade edge should always be removed.

An obtuse angle grind, showing a small bevel.

A lower angle grind showing a larger bevel.

Stropping.

STROPPING

Stropping is something I prefer to do after I have fitted the knife handle as the blade is easier to control. If instead I were doing it before fitting the handle I would use a dummy handle (a bit of wood jammed onto the tang) or I would use a hand vice.

I strop on a leather belt fixed to a piece of wood that has had Autosol and some mineral oil rubbed into it. Some others use green or blue stropping compound rubbed into the leather, but I prefer the lubricating and polishing properties of oil and Autosol. The leather has a little give in it and that is perfect to follow the angle of the slight convex grind left by sharpening on a slack belt.

The purpose of stropping is twofold. Through it we are both polishing the very final angle of the cutting edge and bending the edge burr backwards and forwards until it fatigues and breaks off. The action is very similar to that of bending a metal coat hanger back and forth until it eventually breaks.

It is good practice to get an initial sharpness reference before stropping. I find that cutting clean and dry A4 printer paper gives a very useful guide of sharpness as the fibre strands in the paper cling to any residual burr and indicate the sharpness and toothiness of the blade. If the blade will not cut the edge of the paper, force the tip through the middle of the sheet to get some idea of the sharpness of the blade.

There is a trick to cutting paper that is especially useful for thicker blades. Do not hold the blade at 90 degrees to the paper as this forces the knife to push the paper aside. Instead cut it at an angle of 45 degrees and the paper will easily separate. The test then becomes one of knife sharpness and not the blade thickness. If the blade is sharp it will produce a smooth

Holding the blade in a hand vice is a way of stropping before the handle has been fitted.

Cutting paper on the edge or with the tip of the blade is a way to test a blade's sharpness.

Autosol, strop and mineral oil.

cut without leaving any paper fibres on the edge. If it is blunt it will rip and saw through the paper, leaving traces of paper fibre along the blade edge. Paper is a great way to see if there is any burr left on the blade edge.

I have a very methodical approach to stropping. I strop my blades on a leather strop that has been glued to a piece of wood for a firm backing. The leather has a slight give to it and allows the strop to contour the convex angle of the knife edge. The first step when using the strop is to add some Autosol and mineral oil and smooth this into the belt.

The first step of stropping is to find the final edge angle on the strop. This is done by holding the blade flat on the belt and then starting to push the blade gently forward on the strop. While doing this, slowly lift the angle of the spine of the blade until the edge of the blade tries to cut into the belt. As soon as you feel the blade bite, fix the angle of the blade with your hand on the knife handle. The other hand applies a little pressure and the blade is passed back along the belt away from the edge, making sure that the whole edge of the blade is stropped in each pass.

The edge angle is really important to this method as you want the lowest angle that the edge will bite into the leather. If the angle is too low the strop will just polish the side of the knife. If the angle is too high the strop can blunt the blade. Autosol paste is a very fine abrasive and can blunt the blade as well as sharpen it.

This process is repeated on one side making five passes along the whole blade edge. Turn the blade over, re-establish the bite angle on the other side of the edge and repeat the process with another five passes.

This will offer a good idea of the final sharpening angles. If they are too steep it may be worth going back to the belt grinder and repeating the sharpening steps with the blade presented at a lower angle.

After five strop passes have been completed on each side, repeat the process making a set of four passes on each side, then three passes, then two. When you have finally reached one, perform ten single passes, changing sides between passes. Do this very carefully along the whole edge of the blade, referencing the blade bite angle every time you change from one side to the other. By this point you should be able to feel that the blade is really trying to cut into the leather as you reference the angles.

When ten passes have been completed, I would normally do another ten at a slightly lowered angle to the belt. This final ten passes is to polish the sharpened convex area behind the edge as this is also involved in passing through the material as you cut.

The stropping sequence

- Reference the edge angle on side 1
- Five passes back along the whole blade edge, turn the blade over then
- Reference the edge angle on side 2
- Five passes back along the whole blade edge

Hold the blade flat on the belt.

Lift the angle until it bites into the strop.

Start moving the blade back along the strop.

Fix the angle and move the blade from the tip to the tang back along the strop.

Finish the stropping movement on the tip of the blade.

The angle of the blade on the strop is very important. If is too low you will polish the side of the blade.

With the angle just right the blade edge will be polished.

If the angle is too high you can blunt the blade.

- Reference the edge angle on side 1
- Five passes back along the whole blade edge, turn the blade over then
- Reference the edge angle on side 2
- Four passes back along the whole blade edge

- Reference the edge angle on side 1
- Three passes back along the whole blade edge, turn the blade over then
- Reference the edge angle on side 2
- Three passes back along the whole blade edge

- Reference the edge angle on side 1
- Two passes back along the whole blade edge, turn the blade over then
- Reference the edge angle on side 2
- Two passes back along the whole blade edge

- Reference the edge angle on side 1
- One pass back along the whole blade edge, turn the blade over then
- Reference the edge angle on side 2, turn the blade over then repeat on side 1
- Repeat this process, changing sides each pass
- Repeat until you have ten passes in total, five on each side of the blade.

When these passes have been completed, try the blade again on paper. I also normally use paper to test for any retained burr. The blade should now zip through the paper.

I also test my blades by shaving hair on my arm, as this provides a lot of feedback and there is a big difference between a blade that 'can' shave and one that pops the hairs from your arm!

I find that the convex sharpened edge is a very usable edge for most tasks. It can get very sharp and will hold that sharpness for a long time. To keep the blade in that condition I normally just strop the blade again. If you are going to use a proprietary sharpening system to sharpen your blade, mark the blade edge with permanent marker so you can see where you are sharpening the knife. You are really looking to sharpen the apex angle of the edge.

A sharp blade will slice though paper at an angle and send it flying.

The personal touch – seeing if the blade will shave your arm.

INDEX

accurate bladesmithing 15
air hammers 24
aluminium oxide 20, 21
angle grinder 19
anti-scale compound 63
anvils 13–15
  blade bevelling 47
  edge of 40
  types 13–14
ATP-641 antiscale compound 63
austenite 67
austenitic stainless steel 29
automotive metal polish 76
Autosol 76, 85, 86, 102, 105, 106

belt grinders 18–19, 54, 57
belt grits 20
bench hand tools 21
Birchwood Casey Tru-Oil 96, 97
blacksmith 13
blade bevelling 46–52
bladesmith 13
  anvils 13–15
  cleaning up 68
  forges tools *see* forges tools
  forging *see* forging
  hammers 15–17
  heat treatment 63–72
  materials *see* materials
  stump anvil 14
  thickness 74
  tongs 18
  vices 18
blank blade billet 37
blind operation 57
blown grain 9
bone 32
British industrial forge 8
broach 81
burning on handle 78–81

carbon monoxide (CO) 8, 12
carbon steel 9, 28
ceramic belts 20
charcoal forge 10
chef's knives 41
cherry red 64
coal forge 10, 35
coarse belt 74
coarser grit 54
  scratches 76, 77
coke forge 8–10, 35
colour temper charts 69
convex edge profile 100
correct distal taper 46
Curie point of the steel 66
cutler's resin to fix handles 94–98
cutthroat razor 99

Damascus steel blades 29–30, 33, 85
digital thermometers 12
discard belts 54
dockyard anvil 13–14
Dremels and pendant grinders 19
drilling
  handle block 79
  reference line for 79

face shield 70
ferrous metals 27–30
  laminated steel 30
  mild steel 30
  pattern-welded/damascus steel 29–30
  stainless steel 29
  steel 27–29
  wrought iron 30
finished tang 40, 43
finish grinding 76
fire extinguisher 67
forge tools
  anvils 13–15
  bench hand tools 21
  gas forges 11–12
  grinders 18–21
  hammers 15–17
  heat-treating oven 21–22
  hydraulic power press 24–25
  McDonald rolling mill 25
  personal protection equipment 23
  quenching oil 22
  solid-fuel forges 7–10
  surface grinder 25
  tongs 18
  types 7
  vices 18
forging
  basic 35–36
  blade bevelling 46–52, 54
  finished blade 51
  preform shape 44–45
  stages 45
  straightening 50, 51
  tang 37–43

gas forges 11–12
  heating the blade in 35
  temperature in 36
grinders 18–21
  angle 19
  belts 18–19, 20
  Dremels and pendant 19–20
  grit belt 20–21
  hand sanding 21
  multiple bevels on 59
  surface 25
grinding blade after heat treatment 73–88
  bent blade 74
  burning on handle 78–81
  coarse belt 74
  finishing process 76
  hand sanding 84–88
  knife profile 73
  linear polishing 82–83
  overheating 75
  purpose of 73
  scratches 76
grinding blade before heat treatment 53–62
  belt 54
  blade heat 55
  blade profile 61
  blade with permanent marker 59
  thickness 53

grinding belts 20
grit belt 20–21, 21

hammers 15–17, 41, 42, 47
handle making 89–98
  barrel shape into 93
  cutler's resin to fix handles 94–98
  final fit up and gluing 94–98
  finished and oiled handle 97
  grinding 90
  pencil lines 92
  shaping 90–93
  simple form 89
hand sanding 21, 81, 83, 84–88
hardening process 63, 67–68
hardy hole 37
hardy tool, sharp and blunt edges of 41
heat-treating ovens 21, 71–72
heat treatment 63–72
  grinding blade after 73–88
  grinding before 53–62
  hardening 63, 67–68
  heat-treating ovens 71–72
  normalising 63, 64–66
  quenching 63, 67–68
  straightening 70
  tempering 63, 69
  thermocycling 63
high-grit paper 96
homemade forges 11
horn 32
hot blade tang 95
hydraulic power press 24–25

Industrial Revolution 10

Kevlar gloves 102
knife blades 69, 73

laminated steel 30
latex belt cleaner 91
leg vice 18
linear polishing 81, 82–83
London pattern anvil 13

magnet, testing with 65
martensite 67
martensitic stainless steels 29
materials
  ferrous metals 27–30
  non-ferrous metals 31
  organic 32–34
  tang 37–43
McDonald rolling mill 25
mechanical hammers 24
mild steel 8, 9, 30
monkey-tail tongs 38, 39

neutral zone 10
non-ferrous metals 31
normalising process 63, 64–66
notched push stick 61

obtuse angle grind 104
organic materials 32–34
oxypropane torch, heating tang with 79

pattern-welded steel 29–30, 33
pearlite 67
personal protection equipment (PPE) 23
personal touch 109
polishing wheels 82
Portsmouth pattern anvil 13
power hammer 24
pre-cut blocks for handles 32
pre-heat-treatment grinding 46
principal edge geometry variations 99
profile grinding 61
push stick 60, 61
  notched 61
  tang and blade using 60

quenching oil 22, 63, 67–68

reference line for drilling 79
Renaissance Wax 96
rolling mill 25

safety glasses 70
sandpaper 84, 93
San Mai 30
saw doctor's anvil 14
scratches 76, 77
shaped ceramic belts 20
sharpening 99–109
Sheffield toolmaker's anvil 13
silent killer 12
soapstone 38
solid-fuel forges 7–10
  charcoal forge 10
  coal forge 10
  coke forge 8–10
sparks 8
stainless steels 29
  austenitic 29
  martensitic 29
steel 27–29, 63, 66
  chasing shadows out of 65
  with engineer's chalk 42
  large and small grain in 64
straightening process 70
stropping 104–109
  sequence 106–109
stump anvils 14
surface grinder 25
Swan Portaforge 11

tang 37–43
  and blade 58, 60
  burning on handle 78
  heating with oxypropane torch 79
  hole 79
temperature-controlled oven 69
tempering 69
  temperatures for different knives 69
thermocouple 12
thermocycling process 63, 64–66
three-layer steel 30
tip grinding 56
  hand position for 57
tongs 18
traditional Sheffield bladesmith's anvil 14
type K thermocouple 12, 69

variable frequency drive 77
vices 18, 50
  straightening the blade in 70

wax polishing 96
wood 32
wood dust 90
woodworking chisel 99
wrought iron 30

First published in 2024 by
The Crowood Press Ltd
Ramsbury, Marlborough
Wiltshire SN8 2HR

enquiries@crowood.com
www.crowood.com

© Owen Bush 2024

All rights reserved. No part of this publication may be reproduced or transmitted in any form or by any means, electronic or mechanical, including photocopy, recording, or any information storage and retrieval system, without permission in writing from the publishers.

British Library Cataloguing-in-Publication Data
A catalogue record for this book is available from the British Library.

ISBN 978 0 7198 4447 8

The right of Owen Bush to be identified as author of this work has been asserted by him in accordance with the Copyright, Designs and Patents Act 1988.

Disclaimer
Safety is of the utmost importance in every aspect of blacksmithing and metalworking. When using tools, always follow closely the manufacturer's recommended procedures. However, the author and publisher cannot accept responsibility for any accident or injury caused by following the advice given in this book.

Photographs by Gavin Bush
Typeset by Envisage IT
Cover design by Bluegecko
Printed and bound in India by Thomson Press India Ltd.

A note from the author

By the time this book comes out I will have been making knives for thirty years. During that time I have found the whole subject of knife making to be a huge field of study, ranging from smelting to Damascus steel, axes to swords, kitchen knives to seax. I have studied, researched, made many knives and taught a lot of knife-making classes.

Being a bladesmith has kept my life interesting and full of challenges, provided me with a living and introduced me to lots of talented makers, many of who have become good friends. The craft of bladesmithing has become a lifelong passion, reflected in my motto: Forging Soul Into Steel.

When I started writing this book it soon became evident that I had to simplify the text. This book has accordingly been written with that in mind. It shows one way to make a knife, the way I teach in my knife-making classes. I have tried to go into this simple method of knife making in as much detail as I can, and as such it should be used as a thorough introduction to the wider craft.

I hope you enjoy reading it and that some of you will be inspired to make it the beginning of a lifelong passion of their own.